The Swabian War of 1499

The first confrontation between Landsknechts and the Swiss

Albert Winkler

Helion & Company Limited
Unit 8 Amherst Business Centre
Budbrooke Road
Warwick
CV34 5WE
England
Tel. 01926 499 619
Email: info@helion.co.uk
Website: www.helion.co.uk
X, formerly Twitter: @helionbooks
Visit our blog © Helion and Company 2024

Published by Helion & Company 2024
Designed and typeset by Mary Woolley, Battlefield Design (www.battlefield-design.co.uk)
Cover designed by Paul Hewitt, Battlefield Design (www.battlefield-design.co.uk)

Text © Albert Winkler 2024
Illustrations © as individually credited
Colour artwork by Giorgio Albertini © Helion & Company 2024
Maps by Anderson Subtil © Helion & Company 2024

Every reasonable effort has been made to trace copyright holders and to obtain their permission for the use of copyright material. The author and publisher apologise for any errors or omissions in this work and would be grateful if notified of any corrections that should be incorporated in future reprints or editions of this book.

ISBN 978-1-804515-54-9

British Library Cataloguing-in-Publication Data.
A catalogue record for this book is available from the British Library.

All rights reserved. No part of this publication may be reproduced, stored in a retrieval system, or transmitted, in any form, or by any means, electronic, mechanical, photocopying, recording or otherwise, without the express written consent of Helion & Company Limited.

For details of other military history titles published by Helion & Company Limited contact the above address or visit our website: http://www.helion.co.uk.

We always welcome receiving book proposals from prospective authors.

Contents

Introduction   v

1   Swiss Weapons and Armour   11
2   The Swiss at War   33
3   Background and Causes of the Swabian War   36
4   The Swabian War   46
5   Fighting a Costly War   50
6   Conclusion   107

Colour Plates Commentary   108
Bibliography   111

Introduction

In 1499, a major war took place between the Swiss cantons and their Confederates and the Imperial forces and their allies led by the Emperor Maximilian I. Some of the area of southern Germany facing the Swiss Confederation is known as Swabia, and thus the conflict is often known as the Swabian War in Switzerland and as the Swiss War in Germany. The war is important for its impact on the history of warfare and the development of infantry. The Swiss were among the first to develop a true tactical infantry, known for its ability to manoeuvre successfully in advance and retreat and over rough terrain, while keeping its fighting formation. Yet by the time of the Swabian War, the Germans had also developed infantry along the Swiss model, and the conflict witnessed one of the first times when two competent bodies of infantry met on the field of battle in the early modern era.

Sallet by German armourer Matthes Deutsch, Bavaria, c. 1490. Possibly for use in a tournament. (Metropolitan Museum of Art, Bashford Dean Memorial Collection, Bequest of Bashford Dean, 1928)

The war lasted only about seven months in total, and the campaigning took place largely on the border areas of Switzerland with what is now South Germany, Liechtenstein, and Austria, especially in the modern Swiss border cantons of Solothurn, Thurgau, St Gallen and Graubünden (Grisons). The war has a reputation for ferocity, and witnesses to the conflict stated it was especially 'fierce' and 'deadly'. The contemporary Swabian historian, Johannes Nauclerus, said that the conflict was 'most savage' (*atrocissimum*), and he maintained that so many people had not been killed in the area where the fighting took place in more than 100 years.[1]

---

1 [Johannes Nauclerus], *Chronicon Iohannes Naucleri* (Coloniae [Cologne]: Publisher unknown, 1564), vol. 2, p.514a.

THE SWABIAN WAR OF 1499

A participant in the war, the German humanist Willibald Pirckheimer, called the hostilities the greatest and most pernicious conflict of his generation, or that of his father, had ever experienced. He added that the struggle was the greatest and most lamentable of its kind not only because of the huge numbers of troops involved but also because of the ferocity of the battles and the many costly skirmishes, driven by the mutual hatred of the competing forces.[2]

More recent researchers, Lina Hug and Richard Stead, have attempted to give specific numbers to the destruction and deaths in the war. 'The German territory beyond the Rhine had been wasted; two thousand villages and castles had been destroyed, and twenty thousand soldiers killed.'[3] While this estimate of the number of deaths may be quite reasonable, the figure of the destruction of so many small towns might be too large. If the destruction had reached those numbers, perhaps half of the villages in the Holy Roman Empire would have been lost. Even if these figures have been exaggerated, the overestimation is understandable in view of the extensive destruction of the war.

While soldiers had fought on foot throughout the Middle Ages, they were largely deployed in defensive roles, and their effectiveness in battle was limited. They were generally only minor threats to the heavily-armoured cavalry which dominated many battlefields of the era. Yet starting at the end of the thirteenth century, infantry became increasingly proficient on the field of battle. Among the early successes were the Scots under William Wallace at the Battle of Sterling Bridge in 1297 in which an infantry charge decided the engagement before the enemy cavalry could be properly deployed. The Scots soon after used the schiltron which was a formation of men armed with pikes arrayed in close square formations. Unfortunately for the Scots, the English yeomen, wielding the highly effective longbow, cut them down in many subsequent engagements, thus leaving the development of infantry to other peoples and nations.

English longbowmen were superb troops who fought on foot throughout the fourteenth and fifteenth centuries. These longbowmen were also very effective in fighting the heavily-armoured French knights and men-at-arms during the Hundred Years' War, including at the Battles of Crecy (1346), Poitiers (1356), and Agincourt (1415). Despite their effectiveness in combat, the longbowmen had little skill in manoeuvre. In fact, their tactical deployment was often little more than walking to within shooting range of their adversaries. True disciplined infantry, with the skill to advance and

---

2   [Willibald Pirckheimer], *Wilibald Pirckheimers Schweizerkrieg: nach Pirckheimers Autographum im Britischen Museum*, herausgegeben von Karl Rück (München: K. Akademie, 1895), p.32. Hereafter cited as Pirckheimer, *Schweizerkrieg*, Latin. See also [Willibald Pirckheimer (German translation by Ernst Münch)], *Bilibald Pirkheimers Schweizerkrieg*, (Basel: Schweighauser'schen Buchhandlung, 1826), p.74. Hereafter cited as Pirckheimer, *Schweizerkrieg*, German.
3   Lina Hug and Richard Stead, *Switzerland* (New York: G.P. Putnam's Sons, 1920), p.236.

INTRODUCTION

retreat while keeping their tactical formation, would only develop later and elsewhere.

By the end of the fifteenth century, the cantons of the Swiss Confederation had enjoyed almost complete autonomy from the neighbouring feudal powers for generations. During the fourteenth and fifteenth centuries, the Swiss cantons were beset by external threats to their security, independence, and existence. The largest single menace to Swiss independence in these centuries was the Habsburg family, who controlled many of the areas bordering on Swiss lands. This royal family controlled their holdings by a monarchical authority and a social structure which kept many of their subject peoples as unfree serfs.

The Swiss autonomy or self-rule allowed them to develop unusual social and political institutions. In many instances, democracies, controlled by free men from the lower classes, ruled these cantons. The common people often enjoyed many personal freedoms such as social mobility, the right to own property, and the right to bear arms, which were unusual and highly coveted in the Middle Ages. To a large extent, the Swiss, also known as *Eidgenossen* or Confederates, owed the creation and maintenance of their democracy and freedom to their military competence, which met all external threats.

In these two centuries, the Swiss developed a military system that became among the most respected in Europe. In the fourteenth century through to the middle of the fifteenth century, the Swiss developed from mountain ambushers, as was the case at the Battle of Morgarten in 1315,[4] to infantry proficient in nearly every tactical operation of the age as demonstrated during many military actions of the Burgundian War from 1474 to 1477. The Swiss proved to be among the first genuine tactical infantry in Europe since the fall of the Roman Empire capable of complex and challenging manoeuvres including strategic retreating, keeping unit cohesiveness in difficult situations and over rough terrain, and in dealing most effectively with heavy feudal cavalry.[5] The increased effectiveness of infantry eventually replaced much of the heavy feudal cavalry on the battlefields of Europe. Heavily-armoured cavalry gradually disappeared to be replaced by more lightly-armoured cavalry that relied largely on mobility for their effectiveness, and infantry were well on the road to the development that leads to the modern age.

After the brilliant Swiss victory at the Battle of Murten in 1476, the states of Europe developed a great interest in the Confederates' military prowess.[6] When the French took a contingent of Swiss mercenaries into

---

4   Albert Winkler, 'The Battle of Morgarten: an Essential Incident in the Founding of the Swiss State,' *Swiss American Historical Society Review*, volume 44, no.3, November 2008 (Provo: BYU Scholars Archive 2010), pp.3–25.
5   P. Wilhelm Sidler, *Die Schlacht am Morgarten*, (Zürich: Orel Füssli, 1910), pp.126–9.
6   Albert Winkler, 'The Battle of Murten: The Invasion of Charles the Bold and the

THE SWABIAN WAR OF 1499

Italy in 1495, the armies of Europe got a closer look at the Confederates, and many other armed forces subsequently began to copy their tactics. The Swabians, in the areas of the Holy Roman Empire near the Swiss border, were among the first to try to duplicate the Confederates' military. Anxious to test their nearly identical military force against their old enemies, the Swabians got their opportunity to fight the Swiss in the Swabian War of 1499.

Despite the significance of the Swiss military, the topic needs more careful examination. Although the Swiss chroniclers and contemporary observers were very prolific in recording the activities and character

Armour for a horse and man for field use. A very rare example of an almost complete suit of horse armour. Made in Landshutt by Matthes Deutsch, active c. 1485 to 1505. (Philadelphia Museum of Art, Gift of Athena and Nicholas Karabots and The Karabots Foundation, 2009, 2009-117-20)

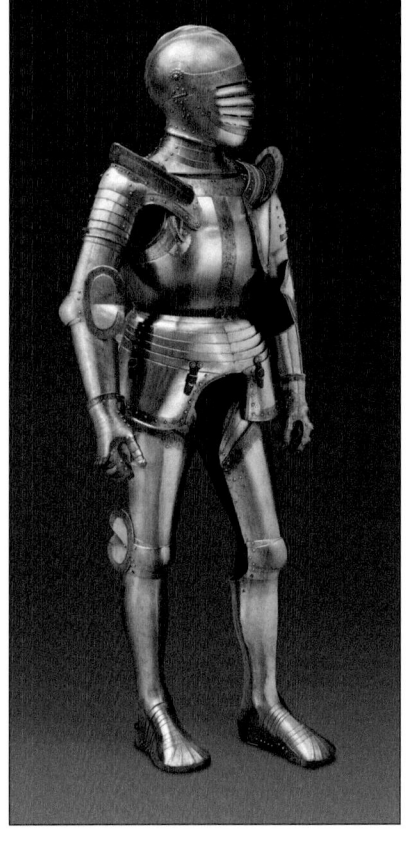

Survival of the Swiss States,' *Swiss American Historical Society Review*, volume 46, no.1 (Feb. 2010), pp.8–34.

of the Confederate military, modern researchers have often overlooked these accounts in favour of foreign, and often less reliable, records. A close examination of the Swiss is long overdue. There are also very few narrative studies on the Swabian War in English. Aside from my preliminary work in this area, only Thomas A. Brady and Tom Scott stand out, but each is fairly short and superficial.[7]

Among the most noteworthy studies in English on Swiss medieval warfare in general are Charles Oman's *A History of the Art of War in the Middle Ages* and *A History of the Art of War in the Sixteenth Century*.[8] Oman's accounts of battles are reasonably accurate even though his descriptions often do not represent the best scholarship available today. His works cover many highlights of Swiss warfare, but he entirely overlooks the Swabian War, and his analyses are often mired in the mistakes of other authors. Oman relies heavily on Machiavelli for insights into the Swiss even though the great Florentine political theorist has long been discredited because his knowledge of the facts of Swiss warfare was meagre.[9] Oman further looks to Carl von Elgger for many details.[10] However, Oman fails to accept Elgger's conclusions and analyses of the Swiss, and his works tend to be superficial. For example, he mistakenly brands the Swiss as being excessively brutal and cruel without attempting to examine their conduct more closely.

Hans Delbrück's extensive four volume work *Geschichte der Kreigskunst* has been recently translated into English. Volume three, *Medieval Warfare*, has sections that deal with the Swiss.[11] Delbrück's study is relatively extensive, and it addresses a wide-range of topics, but his work has been criticised for its anti-Swiss bias including its obvious distortions of the numbers in the armies to make the Confederates appear to have often outnumbered their adversaries when the reverse was almost always the case. Furthermore, Delbrück perpetuated myths about the Swiss military without adequately exploring these issues.[12]

---

7 Thomas A. Brady, *Turning Swiss Cities and Empire, 1450–1550* (New York: Cambridge, 1985), pp.57–72 and Tom Scott, *The Swiss and their Neighbours, 1460–1560: Between Accommodation and Aggression* (Oxford: Oxford University Press, 2017), pp.31–33.
8 Charles Oman, *A History of the Art of War in the Middle Ages* vol. 2 1278–1485 (New York:, Franklin, 1924) and *A History of the Art of War in the Sixteenth Century* (London: Methuen, 1937).
9 Martin Hobohm, *Machiavellis Renaissance der Kriegskunst* (Berlin: Karl Curtius, 1913), p.190.
10 Carl von Elgger, *Kriegswesen und Kriegskunst der Schweizerischen Eidgenossen im XIV, XV. und XVI Jahrhundert* (Lucerne: Militärisches Verlagsbureau, 1873).
11 Hans Delbrück, *Geschichte der Kriegskunst im Rahmen der Politischen Geschichte*, vol. 3 (Berlin: Stilke, 1923) and (Walter J. Renfroe, Jr, trans.) *History of the Art of War* vol. 3 *Medieval Warfare* (Lincoln: University of Nebraska Press, 1990), pp.545–656.
12 Walther Hadron, 'Neues zur Laupenschlacht,' *Blätter für Bernischen Geschichte, Kunst und Altertumskunde* 3 Jahrgang Heft 2 (May 1907), pp.120–125.

THE SWABIAN WAR OF 1499

Other works of value in German include Elgger, perhaps the best analytical study, which takes in the entire scope of the late medieval and renaissance Swiss military, providing numerous details to support his arguments. Other important academic studies include works by Eugen von Frauenholz, Walter Schaufelberger, Albert Sennhauser, and Christian Padrutt.[13] Emil Frey's *Die Kriegstaten der Schweizer dem Volk Erzält* is to date the most comprehensive narrative study.[14] In this huge volume, Frey describes the entire sweep of the history of the Swiss at war from antiquity to the twentieth century, including lengthy accounts of nearly every Confederate military action. A more recent narrative study is Hans Rudolf Kurz's *Schweizerschlachten*.[15]

The Swabian War is a convenient reference point to examine the Swiss and the development of early modern infantry. The Confederate military system was mature by this point. Also, the documentation of the conflict is extensive. Contemporaries and participants carefully recorded the frequent raids and military operations of the War, which present sufficient record to be able to review the Confederates and their enemies in some depth. In this study, the character of the Swiss military will be discussed, questions such as the infamous Swiss brutality will be examined, and the Confederates will be shown in action in the major engagements of the war. This study will further attempt to dispel misunderstandings about the Swiss military and society and to bring them out of the realm of obscurity.

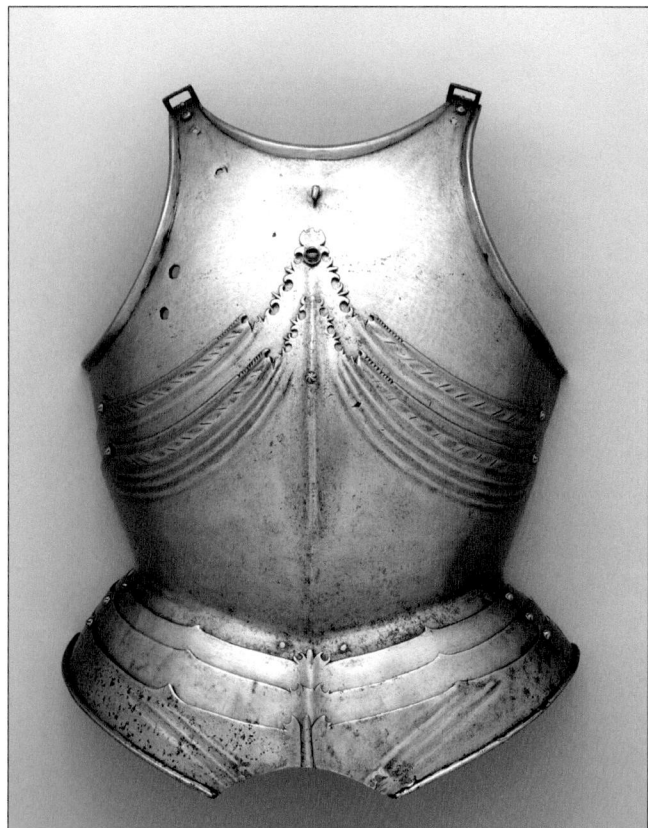

German or Austrian Breastplate c. 1480. (Metropolitan Museum of Art, Bashford Dean Memorial Collection, Bequest of Bashford Dean, 1928)

---

13 Eugen von Frauenholz, *Das Heerwesen der Schweizer Eidgenossenschaft* (München: Beck, 1936); Walter Schaufelberger, *Die alte Schweizer und sein Kreig: Studien zur Kreigführung vornehmlich in 15. Jahrhundert* (Zürich: Europa, 1952); Albert Sennhauser, *Hauptmann und Führung in Schweizerkrieg des Mittelalters* (Zürich: Fretz und Wasmuth, 1965); and Christian Padrutt, *Staat und Krieg im alten Bünden* (Zürich: Fretz und Wasmuth, 1965).

14 Emil Frey, *Die Kriegstaten der Schweizer dem Volk Erzält* (Neuenburg: F. Bahn, 1904).

15 Hans Rudolf Kurz, *Schweizerschlachten* (Bern: Francke, 1962).

1

Swiss Weapons and Armour

By 1499, the Swiss military had proved itself on numerous battlefields and operations. The Confederates had an impressive string of victories to their credit covering several generations, and they were among the most experienced and successful soldiers of their age. Their victories during the Burgundian Wars of 1474–1477 had proved their abilities to all of Europe and the Swiss had earned a great deal of respect and praise. The Confederate successes and reputation for near invincibility came after their adoption and skilful use of the pike and halberd.[1]

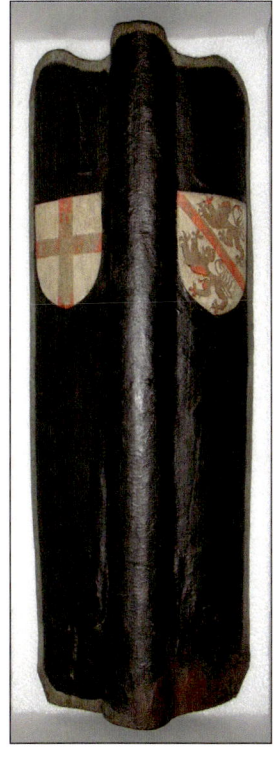

Swiss Pavise, late fifteenth century (Metropolitan Museum of Art Gift of William H. Riggs, 1913)

Swiss Pavise, late fifteenth century. (Metropolitan Museum of Art Gift of William H. Riggs, 1913)

---

1   Frey, *Kriegstaten*, p.477.

THE SWABIAN WAR OF 1499

The Swiss were expected, most frequently, to arm themselves and they usually procured and maintained their own weapons. When any region or area was added to the Confederation, it was expected to adopt the same or similar military requirements as the earlier members of that coalition.[2] The men usually kept their weapons in their home, and these were considered personal property, but as instruments of war were subject to controls and periodic checks by government officials, and strict rules regulated the storage and care of the weapons. At the risk of destruction or confiscation of personal property, the individual was obligated to ensure that his equipment was kept in good condition. This meant keeping all metal free from rust, all edges sharp, and all wood unbroken and free from rot. Weapons and armour were to be kept within the canton, and their sale or loan outside of the canton were strictly forbidden.[3]

The number and type of weapons varied according to the owner's wealth. The wealthier were expected to have the most elaborate armour and the most expensive weapons, yet even the poorest man had to at least have a halberd. If a man was considered wealthy he was expected to purchase his own armour. If he was considered very rich he was expected to buy enough armour for two men. Some weapons, such as cannon and surplus weapons and armour, were owned by the canton and kept in armouries, and there were armouries in nearly every Swiss city. These were large public buildings that were subject to yearly inspection and were conveniently located so the material in them could be easily retrieved in an emergency.[4]

The Confederates were considered master weapon-makers, and their weapons were both well-made and effective.[5] The Swiss soldier carried several weapons, typically a primary weapon for combat as well as a number of secondary ones. The principal weapons were the pike, the halberd, an arquebus, or, infrequently, a two-handed sword.

Early in the fifteenth century a pike three metres in length was introduced from Italy to the Swiss cantons. The weapon was designed to stop cavalry charges, but after the Swiss defeat at the Battle of Arbedo in 1422, it was clearly shown that a longer pike would be more effective in dealing with heavy cavalry, and the long pike soon became the most important weapon used by the Swiss in dealing with mounted 'knights'. The pike was made of ash wood and was usually about five and a half metres long with a point made of steel. The pike was cumbersome to carry and to wield, but it was well-designed to receive the shock of an attacking force composed of heavily-armoured cavalry.[6]

The halberd was among the earliest weapons used by the Swiss, and was wielded by these mountain peoples long before the formation of the Swiss

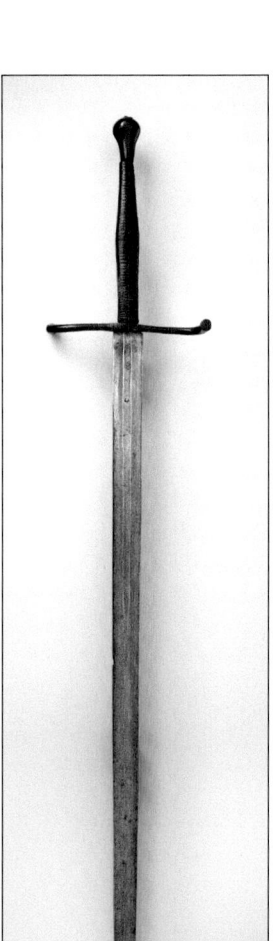

German hand and a half sword c. 1500-1520 (Metropolitan Museum of Art, The Sulzberger Foundation Inc. and Helmut Nickel Gifts)

2   Frey, *Kriegstaten*, p.475.
3   Elgger, *Kriegswesen*, p.81 and Frey, *Kriegstaten*, p.474.
4   Elgger, *Kriegswesen*, pp.82–3 and pp.90–91.
5   Frey, *Kriegstaten*, p.476.
6   Elgger, *Kriegswesen*, 91–2 and Oman, *Art of War*, vol. 2, pp.263–4.

SWISS WEAPONS AND ARMOUR

Confederation in the traditional foundation date of 1291. The halberd was one and half to two and a half metres long and was made of ash wood and steel. The head of the halberd was shaped like a single-bladed axe with a spear point at the top. By the fifteenth century, a hook had been placed at the back of the axe blade. The hook was designed to catch riders and to pull them off their horses, the axe blade was to cut, and the spear point was used for thrusting.[7]

Head of a Swiss halberd, early sixteenth century. (Metropolitan Museum of Art, Gift of William H. Riggs, 1913)

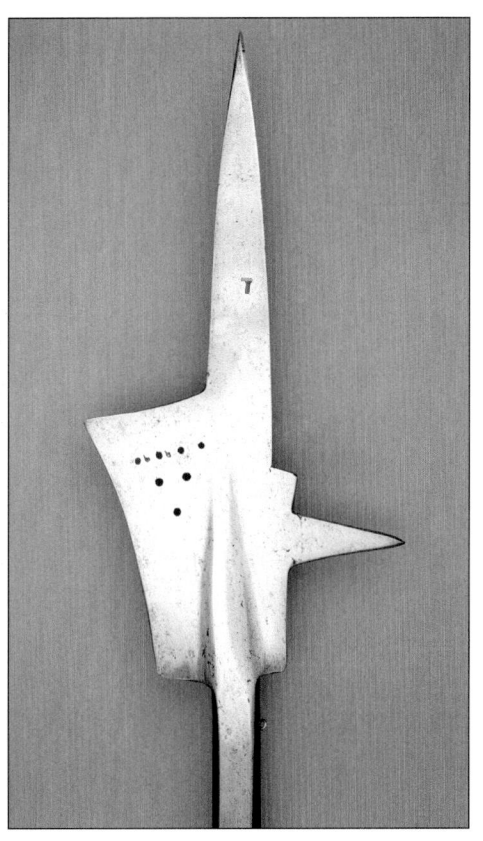

Head of a Swiss halberd, c. 1450. (Metropolitan Museum of Art, Gift of William H. Riggs, 1913)

The development of the arquebus, or harquebus, and other forms of firearms often called *handbüchse* (hand cannons) in the late fifteenth century increased the fighting capabilities of infantry. In many ways, these firearms were an improvement over either the crossbow or the longbow. The arquebus was not as accurate or as rapid firing as these stringed weapons, but the firearms often had significant penetration against plate armour, and they required less skill from the user in comparison to the

---

7   Frey, *Kriegstaten*, p.476.

THE SWABIAN WAR OF 1499

other ranged weapons. Also, the sound of these devices gave their users a greater battlefield presence than the relatively silent stringed weapons. The use of firearms in volley firing also improved their effectiveness, and the psychological impact of the fusillade assured the ascendancy of the hand-held gun.[8] Yet firearms were still in early stages of development, and their effectiveness on the battlefield was limited. While guns could certainly soften up an enemy when used in both attack and defence, they were not yet crucial weapons on the battlefield, and every major engagement of the Swabian War was decided by the infantry assault and hand-to-hand combat. Firearms were most effective when used to defend fortified positions. In those locations made of earth, wood, and stone, guns could be propped on walls meaning they were at rest, which greatly increased the accuracy of the weapons when they were discharged.

Sallet helmet from Nuremburg, c. 1490. The wide, flat comb indicates that this helmet is a late example dating to the end of the fifteenth century. An armourer's mark in the shape of a horseshoe enclosing a letter, suggests the helmet's maker may have been Hans Grünewalt (c. 1440–1503). (Metropolitan Museum of Art, Bashford Dean Memorial Collection, bequest of Bashford Dean, 1928)

The arquebus was the weapon that superseded the crossbow as the main ranged weapon of the Swiss. These 'hand cannons' shot a projectile of lead and had a maximum range of about 150 to 200 paces, but they were only accurate at much shorter distances. The early versions of the arquebus were heavy to carry, slow to load, and had a considerable recoil. By the end of the fifteenth century, the barrel of the arquebus was fixed in a wooden stock that was pressed against the right shoulder when firing. The touch hole, where the powder was ignited, had previously been on the top of the barrel, but it had been moved to the right side to facilitate easier aiming. The spark to ignite the powder was from a smouldering cord (or match) that was commonly held in the right hand or placed on a 'hammer-like' apparatus, giving the weapon the name matchlock, which was dropped by means of a lever, forcing the spark into the hole to ignite the powder. When men carrying arquebuses were on the march, the smouldering cord was usually slung around their shoulders like bandoliers, and the men took care to make sure the cord remained lit.[9]

After the Burgundian Wars of 1474 to 1477, the 5 or 6 foot two-handed sword enjoyed some popularity, but the weapon was considered inferior to the halberd because it was too short to stab with effectively. The Swiss Federal Diet, meeting in Lucerne at the outset of the Swabian War, forbade the use of these swords as a general weapon on 22 March 1499.[10]

---

8   Oman, *Art of War*, vol. 2, pp.268–9.
9   Frey, *Kriegstaten*, p.480 and Elgger, *Kriegswesen*, p.97–98.
10 Elgger, *Kriegswesen*, p.94 and Frey, *Kriegstaten*, p.479.

SWISS WEAPONS AND ARMOUR

Besides their main weapon, the Swiss usually carried other secondary ones. A short sword with a rounded tip was carried on the left side, and a dagger with a sharp point on the right. These weapons were often used when opposing forces became so closely entwined with the Swiss that the mass of men made it impossible to use the long pikes or halberds effectively. In such a situation, a short weapon gave its user a marked advantage.[11]

A preferred, and considered optimum, ratio of pikemen to halberdiers was 8 to 1, which was thought necessary to ensure maximum efficiency on the battlefield. The tactics thus called for a large number of pikemen and a relatively small number of halberdiers, but the popularity of the shorter weapon made these ratios difficult to achieve. The halberd was lighter, cheaper, and less cumbersome than the long, heavy pike, making practising and marching much easier, and pikemen were also often more encumbered with armour. As a result, it was necessary to induce more men to wield the longer weapon. Thus, pikemen were frequently paid more than halberdiers, but when monetary inducements were insufficient, the various cantons ordered men to carry pikes. One such order from Bern in 1515 stated: 'Whoever can carry a pike should carry a pike.'[12]

The actual ratio of weapons in the Swiss forces varied: in 1490, of 450 men from Wallisau, an area of Lucerne, 200 carried pikes, 200 halberds, and 50 arquebuses. Lucerne was an extreme example because it, as well as the other cantons of the central areas of the Confederation, had a relatively large contingent of halberdiers among its troops. Early in the sixteenth century, the Swiss armies were composed of about one-sixth armed with arquebuses and less than one-eighth with halberds; this meant that roughly 70 percent of the men carried pikes.[13]

The Swiss also deployed small detachments of cavalry, the wealthiest of all the Swiss soldiery. Men who lived in the cities usually carried arquebuses while the peasants and other rural people wielded either pikes or halberds. In the fifteenth century, even the priests, who accompanied the men into battle, were expected to be armed with swords to avoid scorn from the troops. Of course, church law forbade priests from shedding blood, so the weapons were only for show. The men often sought to capture weapons and banners as prizes from the field of battle, and the reports of victory in the field almost always included the careful numbering and listing of captured enemy artillery pieces and flags.[14]

---

11 Elgger, *Kriegswesen*, p.94.
12 Elgger, *Kriegswesen*, pp.103–104.
13 Elgger, *Kriegswesen*, p.56 and pp.105–106.
14 Frey, *Kriegstaten*, p.475 and Elgger, *Kriegswesen*, p.83 and pp.106–107.

THE SWABIAN WAR OF 1499

Bad War, attributed to Hans Holbein the Younger (c. 1497-1543)(Albertina Museum, Vienna)

How some of the weapons were wielded at this period of time remains unclear. The available information comes largely from contemporary drawings and from accounts recorded at a later date, and many aspects remain obscure. For example, the men wielding the halberd could have used it to thrust, much like a spear, or they may have swung it like a battle axe. As skilful soldiers, they may have used the weapon in more than one manner depending on the nature of the combat. Apparently, the halberd was a poor defensive weapon, because even a skilful user would have difficulty in warding off blows with it, and it could be used more effectively in an offensive role. While men could advance and thrust with the pike, its length made it most suitable to resist cavalry charges. No matter how these weapons were used, it may be surmised from their success in battles and on campaigns that the Swiss showed a high degree of professionalism and considerable skill in their weapons' use.[15]

Practice and Service

Another perplexing question remains on the frequency and nature of the practice the Swiss undertook with their weapons. However, there is little information on how the men drilled or practised their combat formations. Possibly, such activities were so common that they attracted little attention from contemporary observers, but there is evidence that the children in the Swiss cantons practised military marching and manoeuvres from a young age. Swiss youths and boys were clearly interested in the affairs of men, and these children were often engaged in copying their elders, and it was natural that in their play boys would copy the activities of adults. During

---

15   Elgger, *Kriegswesen*, pp.260–264.

the Burgundian Wars, in the spring of 1475, a military contingent from Bern, accompanied by forces from Lucerne, was returning from one of several major campaigns of the war in the Vaud region. As they approached the city of Bern, the men of Lucerne were greeted by a delegation from their home canton. These representatives were accompanied by 400 'young boys' (*iunger knaben*) who all carried weapons – pikes, arquebuses, crossbows, et cetera. With these weapons, each boy had a banner, or simply a small flag attached to a pole. These flags were painted with the emblems of Bern, Lucerne, and other Confederate cantons, but most displayed Lucerne's insignia. These youths marched in good order with their own leaders towards the returning men whom they greeted, giving them a short speech in unison.[16]

Most of the Swiss wore no uniforms, preferring to wear simple everyday clothing, either out of choice or because of the additional expense of buying specific attire. When the Confederates wore uniforms, this clothing was frequently in the colours of the canton from which the wearer originated. The Swiss wore white crosses either on their stockings, shoulders, or hats to distinguish themselves from their enemy. The use of armour varied from none to a complete covering consisting of a helmet, a coat of mail, back and breast plates, leg guards, and metal gauntlets. Pikemen were most often well-armoured. The men wielding the arquebuses had perhaps no more than a helmet, and the halberdiers were likewise less well-protected, mostly lacking any defensive armour.[17]

Each soldier was supposed to carry a haversack containing oatmeal for 14 days as well as salt, bread, cheese, and butter. The only spare article of clothing in this haversack was a new pair of shoes. On marches into enemy territory, the Swiss lived off the land, and foragers often left the column of marching men in search of supplies. A baggage train with tents and other bulky supplies often accompanied the Confederate Army, but the men certainly travelled as lightly as possible to increase their mobility while on the march, particularly on a raid, but if a baggage train slowed the army down it could be left behind to catch up later.[18]

Swiss Artillery

Modern scholars seldom refer to the Swiss as great artillerymen, but in the Swabian War, cannon played a significant role and had a large impact on the outcome of hostilities. In 1499, the Confederates had nearly 1,000 pieces of artillery of various sizes for use in different functions.[19]

---

16 Diebold Schilling (Gustav Tobler, ed.) *Die Berner-Chronik 1468–1484* (Bern: K. J. Wyss, 1897–1901) vol. 2, p.224.
17 Elgger, *Kriegswesen*, pp.91 and 116.
18 Frey, *Kriegstaten*, p.485.
19 Johannes Häne, 'Die Kriegsbereitschaft der alten Eidgnossen,' *Schweizer*

THE SWABIAN WAR OF 1499

The Swiss had captured many artillery pieces in the Burgundian Wars, especially after the battles of Grandson and Murten, both in 1476. As a result of such an abundance, the Swiss progress in the making of cannon was slowed because they had no need to manufacture or purchase them. Cannon were made of either bronze or iron, and shot projectiles of either stone or iron. Artillery pieces were of various sizes and different calibres, and were deployed in variety of circumstances. Large cannon were used to bombard cities and to besiege castles and towns, but they also fired on troops when the opportunity arose. Small artillery pieces were used primarily against armies in the field, but the Swiss often also took them on raids when they could be deployed rapidly to fire on towns and other fortifications.[20]

Many advances were made in cannon manufacture immediately preceding and during the Swabian War, marking it as a turning point in the history of artillery. The Emperor Maximilian took the first steps towards a unified calibre and barrel length during the war. In 1497, burning shells were used that could not be put out with water, and explosive artillery projectiles also found an early use in the conflict. These improvements helped advance the art of war since explosive shells more rapidly reduced fortifications and did greater damage to cavalry or to infantry formations. Burning shells also assured that a town could more easily be set on fire, greatly reducing the length of a siege.[21]

Better artillery tactics were also being employed. Cannon were often all aimed at one point thus increasing their effectiveness, and firing the devices in a cannonade created what seemed to be a solid wall of stone or lead or iron. The impacts of these improvements in artillery and in its tactical use were well demonstrated near the city of Constance, which the Germans used as a fortified base throughout the war. In July 1499 Maximilian marched his army on some Swiss positions nearby. These defensive posts were largely unmanned because the troops were hastening to Gempen where they were to participate in the Battle of Dornach, but 80 cannon were still in position. The artillery pieces fired to such great effect that Maximilian's army was thrown into confusion and withdrew without pressing its attack further.[22]

Artillery could be fired with increasing accuracy and over ever greater distances because of longer barrel lengths and improved powder. When artillery pieces were properly aimed, they could be shot considerable distances night or day. In one instance in the Swabian War, a gun was fired from the fortress at Constance at a group of three Swiss children playing over a mile away. The shot was right on its mark, but it passed harmlessly

---

    Kriegsgeschichte (1915) vol. 3, p.14.
20 E. A. Gessler, *Das schweizerische Geschützwesen zur Zeit des Schwabenkriegs, 1499* (Zürich: Kommissionsverlag Beer & Co., 1927), p.7.
21 Gessler, *Geschützwesen*, pp.16 and 47.
22 Heinrich Brennwald, *Schweizerchronik* (Basel: Basel Buch-und Antiquariatshandlung, 1910), vol. 2, pp.445–7.

between the three hurting none of them.[23] There were a great number of cannon of various calibres at Constance, some of which were large and are believed to have been able to fire a considerable distance.[24] At such distances the cannon no doubt had a high trajectory, shooting much like modern howitzers.

Most of the Swiss heavy cannon were placed in the border areas because of the greater need for protection, and where they would be available to support raids into enemy territory when sufficiently mobile. Cannon had become so critical that on occasion an operation's success or failure depended on the skilful use of artillery. Often Swiss raiders were able to take towns after only a few cannon rounds had been fired. But the weapon still had drawbacks including a slow rate of fire and the difficulty in moving it. Even at the end of the sixteenth century, under ideal circumstances, a large artillery piece could only be fired four times in an hour, and movement over the poor roads common to the age often required much effort and time.[25]

Swiss Infantry Tactics and Tactical Formations

In battle and on the march, the Swiss employed a tight formation called the *haufen* (heap or crowd). The *haufen* was a square with four corners (*viereck*) formed by troops lined up in rows, and the *haufen* may be best translated as a pike square or battle square.[26] The Swiss pike square developed in the fourteenth century and was probably first used at the Battle of Laupen in 1339. There is no evidence that the Swiss developed this formation from reading classical authors, so the early military leaders of the Swiss Confederation must get credit for this tactical structure rather than any scholars who studied antiquity.[27] Even though the *haufen* was a formation similar to the ancient Greek or Macedonian phalanx, neither primary nor secondary Swiss sources call this formation a phalanx.

The Swiss pike square was formed out of small tactical units of 50, 100, 200, or 300 men depending on the area from which the troops originated and the conditions of their recruitment.[28] The military traditions in the various cantons and availability of manpower account for the disparity of sizes. The number of troops designated for special duty, such as garrisoning a fortress, varied in size depending on the numerous differing factors of that duty. The typical small pike square was 25 men wide and 25 men deep, a total of 625 men. This figure was considered the ideal, but there were

---

23   Gerold Edlibach, *Chronik*. (Zürich: Meyer und Zeller, 1847), pp.214.
24   Gessler, *Geschützwesen*, pp.47–8.
25   Elgger, *Kriegswesen*, pp.135–6 and p.139.
26   Johann Lenz, *Der Schwabenkrieg* (Zürich: Orell Füssli, 1849), p.49.
27   Elgger, *Kriegswesen*, pp.104–5.
28   Elgger, *Kriegswesen*, pp.14–15.

THE SWABIAN WAR OF 1499

The Battle near Naples, by Hans Burgkmair, possibly depicting an event from the Third Italian War of 1502–1504. The bloody nature of 'push of pike' is depicted in detail. (Metropolitan Museum of Art, Bequest of Grace M. Pugh, 1985)

many examples of this formation being composed of both fewer and many more men.

The standard Swiss battle deployment consisted of three pike squares, each varying in size, position, and use. The *vorhut* (vanguard or advanced party) was the pike square furthest forward, and it was usually stationed on the right of the other formations. The vanguard was the first pike square to engage the enemy, and it was supposed to penetrate and break the opposing enemy lines if possible. The *vorhut* was often composed of young, unmarried men who were well-armoured and were considered to be the best men available. The largest pike body was the *gewalthaufen* (main or chief formation) where the largest contingent of men was placed, and at times it numbered many thousands. It advanced in the centre, was the heaviest blow the Swiss could throw, and it was always placed at least the distance of an arquebus shot from the vanguard. The *gewalthaufen*, with its pikemen and halberdiers holding their weapons vertically, has been described as resembling a walking forest. The third body was the *nachhut* (rearguard), which was used as the reserve of the army and was often used to protect the baggage train. Most commonly the elderly men were found in the rearguard, and in times of need, members of the baggage train, such as cooks, were found in it.[29]

The pike square consisted of pikemen three or four ranks deep on each side. In the centre of the formation were found ranks of halberdiers. Arquebusiers were not basic to the formation, but were often placed behind the first rank of pikes to shoot at enemy cavalry. When there was little to fear from men on horseback, the arquebusiers were frequently placed in a group separate from the main pike body.[30]

The Swiss had a reputation for being aggressive in battle, and they were most often tactically on the offensive, so the pike squares were used to penetrate enemy formations. The square would advance at a fast pace to the sound of drums and fifes which helped the troops maintain order. It is unclear if the men marched in step even though such a practice would have helped them maintain good order. To retain their formation and provide space for the proper use of their weapons, the men were often stationed with an arm's length, approximately one metre, between them. When the troops reached their enemy, the pikemen were supposed to level their pikes from the vertical to the horizontal and thrust forward to force a hole in the enemy line. Then the halberdiers would rush through the one metre between the pikemen and seek to do as much damage as possible to the enemy, breaking their morale, and cracking their formation.[31]

Nonetheless, it was often the case that the known terrain and position and character of the enemy forces made these tactics unlikely to succeed without some modification. Frequently, the proper ratio of halberdiers, men with firearms, and pikemen needed to carry out these operations was hard to achieve. As a result, these idealised formations would vary as the Swiss commanders attempted to use their available forces to the best advantage. Yet whenever possible, a battle line with three bodies as the core element was used.

A pike square was only effective when order was maintained. Often, it was that discipline and order that brought the Swiss victory, with the relative disorder of their enemy causing them to suffer defeat. The Confederates had an impressive record for keeping their formations while marching over many challenging obstacles and even in the face of heavy fire from enemy artillery. Iron discipline was necessary to keep the men in good order under trying circumstances, and the Swiss were obliged to follow their leaders or face punishment. Any breach of discipline on operations or in combat was tried through the testimony of eyewitnesses, and those guilty of serious crimes could be summarily beheaded. Executions or the threat of capital

---

29 Elgger, *Kriegswesen*, pp.248, 274 and 276–277.
30 Kurz, *Schweizerschlachten*, p.144 and Elgger *Kriegswesen*, p.279.
31 Elgger, *Kriegswesen*, p.278.

punishment must have been common since men designated as executioners frequently accompanied Swiss troops in the field.[32]

The Swiss iron discipline only applied to watch posts and when the army was either in battle or on the march. When not actually fighting or on campaign, the Confederates were often undisciplined and disobedient. Some of the most notorious examples of misconduct came following battles or campaigns when the soldiers plundered and took revenge on their enemies.[33]

Flags and banners often helped the men keep in place and in order within the pike squares. Every district or region had its own banners and flags which were the pride of the populace. Such items were so prized that it was considered an honour to carry them on campaign and into battle. This privilege typically went to 'leaders' of higher status in the army. To prevent a banner's capture often as many as 100 men were assigned to protect it. This practice helped keep order in the pike squares and give the troops a rallying point especially during the confusion of battles. Because the flags and banners were prized booty for an enemy, wild and fierce fights often took place around them. When a flag was captured by the enemy, the new one replacing it was marked with a red cross to denote that it, and its army, had been shamed. That sign of remorse was only removed after the flag had been redeemed by enemy blood in battle.[34]

Whenever overwhelming numbers attacked a Swiss pike square, the formation would cease to move, and the troops would turn their pikes outward to receive attacks from all directions. Everyone in the formation, including the halberdiers, would rush to defend the sides thus leaving the centre hollow. This hollow core gave the formation flexibility, which allowed it to withstand more external shock. The most vulnerable points in the pike square under heavy attack were its corners, so the tendency was to round the corners making the formation appear as a hedgehog or *igel*. The hedgehog was so formidable that it made possible for the Swiss to continue fighting under the most difficult circumstances. There are no examples of a hedgehog being breached in battle after it had been completely formed.[35]

During the Swabian War, the Swiss proved to be very mobile giving them great success through the element of surprise. The Confederates were accustomed to marching all night to reach objectives and then to fall on enemy positions. They were so proficient at such manoeuvres that the German mercenaries at Constance in 1499 feared that the Swiss would

---

32 Delbrück, *Kriegskunst*, vol. 3, p.619 and Häne, 'Kriegsbereitschaft,' p.32.
33 Valerius Anshelm, *Berner-Chronik* (Bern: Wyss, 1886), vol. 2, p.140 and Frey, *Kriegstaten*, p.497.
34 Gessler, *Geschützwesen*, p.76; Elgger, *Kriegswesen*, p.122; and Frey, *Kriegstaten*, pp.487–488.
35 Elgger, *Kriegswesen*, p.281.

SWISS WEAPONS AND ARMOUR

The War in Hainault. Woodcut by Hans Springinklee, depicting the close and bloody nature of the infantry battle of the period. (Courtesy National Gallery of Art, Washington)

attempt to storm that city at night, even though it had high walls and was well defended with a large garrison and many artillery pieces.[36]

Swiss Troops and Leaders

The Swiss relied on a council of war for military leadership. This assembly came from each Swiss canton with troops present and was comprised of experienced military men. Wealth and social position were clearly considerations in the selection of its members, but a man's experience and

---

36   Brennwald, *Schweizerchronik*, vol. 2, p.445.

abilities were also carefully scrutinised. The council of war often directed military affairs and oversaw the overall strategy of the war, but it frequently chose commanders in the field to provide leadership during the actual campaigns.[37]

The Swiss levels of military leadership were far different than the rank structures in modern armies, and any similarity between medieval and modern terms designating leadership is coincidental. The man designated as *hauptmann* (best translated as leader or commander) was the highest Swiss officer, and he was considered so important that a group of men were assigned to protect him. The council of war chose this officer not necessarily for his genius, but for his courage and the ability to understand the troops and the military system. It was expected, in theory at least, that the military structure, and not the abilities of any one man, was the key to victory. Yet the leaders in the field enjoyed great leeway in their decisions and often saw fit to vary the system to meet unforseen circumstances.[38]

Several leaders were typically placed beneath the *hauptmann*, including the men assigned to carry the flags and banners. These men were known as *pannerherren*, as well as *venner* and *venliträger*. Each of these men had responsibilities related to the carrying of one of a number of flags and banners. They should properly be known as the banner or flag carriers. The *pannerherren* usually carried city or regional flags, while the *venner* and *venliträger* carried banners of less significance, which represented smaller numbers of men. Unlike the *hauptmann*, these lower officers were elected by the troops after the forces had assembled. At that time, all the leaders came together and forgave each other all hate and injury and swore loyalty one to another. The lesser leaders and troops swore to follow the higher officers and the higher officers swore to all the men of the army to lead them as well as possible.[39]

Among the officers' most challenging functions was to organise the pike bodies and decide on a course of action and a battle plan when such action was warranted. A pike square was often composed of men who had never seen each other before, and great care had to be taken to assure that the formation was composed of the appropriate ratios of pikemen and halberdiers. The men from the same region and of similar occupations naturally wanted to be positioned with their friends and family members. The leaders often demonstrated considerable skill in organising the pike squares because they were rapidly formed in various battles. The battle plan was usually a product of consultations among the more important leaders of each contingent that comprised the army at that point. These leaders were usually *hauptmänner* (commanders) who came together to form the 'battle council' and to decide jointly on the best course of action. They used the information and intelligence available to them, and they also

---

37 Elgger, *Kriegswesen*, pp.33–34 and 195.
38 Elgger, *Kriegswesen*, pp.204–205.
39 Elgger, *Kriegswesen*, pp.200–201 and Delbrück, *Kriegskunst*, vol. 3, p.620.

carefully considered the abilities of their men. No doubt, the battle plan often came from the ideas and skills of one or more of the most respected and influential leaders on the 'battle council'.

There were numerous lower officers who had specific authority over baggage, food, and artillery. Among these men, the Master of Artillery (*Büchsenmeister*) was often the most respected. The Master of Artillery was the master cannon-maker who served as the chief artillery officer in the field. These leaders were highly skilled and provided expert leadership in directing the use of cannon on military operations. Between campaigns the Master of Artillery also made weapons and powder, and trained men in their maintenance and use.[40]

Swiss troops basically fell into two broad categories, the *landsturm* and the *söldner*. The *landsturm* was the Swiss Militia, and consisted of virtually the entire healthy adult male population. Its function was to protect the local area. This force was called into service whenever an enemy invaded the lands of the Confederation, and it was never used in campaigns outside of the Swiss lands. These fighters saw a great deal of service in the Swabian War, and were used to watch the borders of the Confederation and to resist enemy raids into the Swiss territories.[41]

The men in the Swiss Militia were called to their assembly areas by the use of smoke signals, the ringing of bells, or a flag placed in a stream in the daytime, while fire signals were used at night. Assembly areas were usually at churches, located in or near the centre of towns or villages. Once the men had gathered, the nature of the emergency was explained to them, and some leaders were quickly elected. Any man failing to appear at the designated area could suffer a loss of goods, and his home could also be destroyed as a punishment for the infraction.[42]

The men in the Swiss Militia were responsible for detecting intruders, and for that purpose, numerous watch posts were placed on any avenue of approach that the enemy might use. Watch posts were commonly located on hill tops or near mountain passes, but could be at any place that afforded a good view of the surrounding terrain. The man on watch had to be constantly alert. If anyone fell asleep, laid down his weapon, or failed to wear his equipment, he could be put to death. The Swiss always built some border defences of wood, earth, or stone to prepare their positions in case of attack. Such positions were called *letzi*. Frequently the Swiss used dogs to help watch for the enemy or chase them if needed. Watch posts and border defences often became the scenes of skirmishes with hostile raiders or with larger enemy units, and such obstacles frequently formed the first line of defence. The Confederates had an excellent record of ambushing their enemy while these were seldom successful in doing the reverse. In

---

40 Otto Hess, *Die Fremden Büchsenmeister und Söldner in den Diensten: Der Eidgen-Orte bis 1516* (Dietikon: J. G. Hunndel-Horner, 1919), pp.1–3.
41 Häne, 'Kriegsbereitschaft,' p.27 and Elgger, *Kriegswesen*, p.318.
42 Elgger, *Kriegswesen*, pp.37–8.

part, the credit for such success must go the men who so carefully manned the watch posts.[43]

Another category of men in the military was the *söldner* (soldier) - someone paid for his military service. Strictly speaking, soldiers were only garrison troops guarding city gates and castles and also acting as municipal police. However, the term was often applied to any military personnel aside from the militia. A broad designation often given to any troops in the field was *knechte* (servant or vassal), but more commonly these men were called *freiwillige* (volunteers). These were the men who waged wars outside the borders of the Swiss Confederation, and they were often employed on raids into enemy territories. In the classical battle formation or pike square, the volunteers took positions within the vanguard or *vorhut* of the army. These troops were usually young, vigorous men interested in fame, adventure, and wealth. They were also the men recruited as mercenaries and who served in foreign armies.[44]

The size of all the Swiss forces when mobilised and on campaign remains unclear, but certain estimates can be made. During the late Middle Ages, perhaps as many as 30,000 Swiss were on any military operation at one time on foreign soil. But this estimate refers only to volunteers and does not include the militia. Even though military service began when boys reached their mid-teens, the total army hardly consisted of more than a quarter of the entire population. Taking this into consideration, the Swiss total forces could never have been more than 100,000 men. In practical terms, a plausible number of total mobilisation ranges between 60,000 and 80,000 men.[45]

Yet the Confederates never fielded their total strength during the Swabian War. One contemporary foreign observer, Bernardin de Vegiis, estimated the strength of the Swiss troops deployed from the various cantons and their allies on or near the borders of the Confederation: he listed 6,000 from Bern, Fribourg at 2,000, Lucerne at 3,000, and Zürich at 4,500. He also listed 800 men from Uri, 600 from Unterwalden, 2,400 from Schwyz. 5,000 from Graubünden (Grisons), 400 from Zug, 500 from Glarus, 6,000 from St Gallen, Appenzell, and the Thurgau, 400 from Schaffhausen, 1,800 from Solothurn, and 1,000 from the Wallis. The total was 34,400 men.[46] An anonymous, yet very thorough report, by another contemporary estimated the total Swiss strength deployed at any one time during the war at 20,800 men.[47] Both of these contemporary estimates are plausible depending,

---

43 Elgger, *Kriegswesen*, pp.324–329.
44 Hess, *Büchsenmeister und Söldner*, p.49 and Elgger, *Kriegswesen*, pp.49–50.
45 Häne, 'Kriegsbereitschaft,' p.24 and Delbrück, *Kriegskunst*, vol. 3, p.617.
46 Bernardin de Vegiis an den Herzog von Mailand, 29 April 1499 in Albert Büchi, (ed.) *Aktenstücke zur Geschichte des Schwabenkrieges nebst einer Freiburger Chronik über die Ereignisse von 1499* (Basel: Basler Buch- und Antiquariatshandlung, 1901), p.167.
47 Bericht eines Ungenannten an den Herzog von Mailand 29 May 1499 in

of course, on how many of the men in the militia were included in these numbers.

Swiss Popular Support for Military Service

Swiss men were required to serve in the military from a young age. In times of emergencies, young males could be enrolled in the military as early as age 14, but most commonly they started to serve when 16. From age 16 to 25, the men were considered to be in their prime for military operations and combat. Older men were often used as well, and only the physically unfit were exempt from military duty. Otherwise, everyone served regardless of wealth or station in life, although it was more common to find peasants in the army, because of their greater numbers than those who lived in cities. When a man was placed in the military, he had to swear an oath that he would serve with 'goods and blood' when necessary. Training was often mandatory, but the Swiss rarely considered this duty as a chore, and they were often happy to practice wielding their weapons and marching with others.[48]

Military service was so popular for young boys that they often tried to accompany forces on campaign before they reached the appropriate age because they were anxious to share the fame, fortune, and adventure of military operations. In such instances, it was necessary to forbid them from taking part. Although every male was expected to serve in the military, at times additional men had to be induced when too few volunteers came forward for certain operations. This situation occurred more frequently when mercenary service in foreign lands drained the Swiss manpower. Sometimes, one of two brothers was required to serve or either a father or his son had to report for duty. At times, the widows of men who had fallen in battle would select those who were to replace them. It was possible for a man to pay another to fulfil the man's requirement for military service, but this practice was forbidden by the Federal Diet meeting in Zürich on 16 June 1499. This decree stated that everyone had to serve in person when called, although it remains unclear whether this order was carefully observed, and the wealthy still had the means to pay others to take their place.[49]

Taxes on persons, guilds, and societies pad for and supported the military. A tax was levied on the individual regardless of his ability to pay, and it was collected on a monthly or daily basis. Guilds were often responsible for the recruitment, pay, and support of the troops that they put into the field. If the troops were hired as mercenaries, their employers cared for their needs and

---

    Aktenstücke, pp.539–547.
48 Delbrück, *Kriegskunst*, vol. 3, p.615 and p.622; Häne, 'Kriegsbereitschaft,' p.13; Elgger, *Kriegswesen*, pp.25 and 35.
49 Elgger, *Kriegswesen*, p.61 and Frey, *Kriegstaten*, p.470.

THE SWABIAN WAR OF 1499

Schweizerkrieger. Print by Urs Graf of a Swiss soldier (Wiki Creative Commons)

were required to pay them as well. However, the men often supported themselves from plunder and the taking of booty.[50]

Military service was a popular means of employment for the Swiss, especially as foreign mercenaries, since they lived in a poor country. Such employment could also be very profitable, and once-poor peasants often lived well as elderly men from the rewards received from service as soldiers. Many of these men also used martial activities as an important means of achieving social mobility. Military men frequently found their way onto a seat on a city or cantonal council, and at times a successful military background seemed almost mandatory for many high positions.[51] The Swiss found military activities so profitable that they formed bands of brigands to fight and raid on their own without official sanction, but in which cases, they risked punishment and death as outlaws. The Swiss were very proud of their military, and soldiers were revered and respected people. Songs were composed praising military victories, and the thirst for success, praise, and fame helped motivate these troops to fight well and hard.[52]

The Swiss were very conscientious over their own troops, showing great affection and concern for their welfare. They commonly referred to the care of the wounded as 'holy duty'. After the disastrous defeat at the Battle of Marignano in 1515, the Confederates showed such concern for their own wounded that, while they should logically have been fleeing from a possible enemy pursuit, they returned to the field of battle to carry their wounded and injured men more than a mile to a place where they could be treated.[53]

The Swiss included men who were responsible to care for the wounded on every military expedition. These men were the *feldschere* (barber surgeons) whose only function was to care for wounded and injured. In battle, *feldschere* or doctors put up a flag to indicate where they were working, and they and their assistants tended to the wounded as an immediate aid whenever needed. After treatment in the field, the wounded were sent home where they were given care and monetary compensation during their convalescence. If the wounded man lost a limb or was maimed for life, he

---

50   Delbrück, *Kriegskunst*, vol. 3, p.616 and Elgger, *Kriegswesen*, p.169.
51   Hobohm, *Renaissance der Kriegskunst*, p.171 and Elgger, *Kriegswesen*, p.227.
52   Frey, *Kriegstaten*, p.472 and Elgger, *Kriegswesen*, pp.234–5.
53   Frey, *Kriegstaten*, p.491.

would be cared for at canton or community expense for the rest of his life. If a man was permanently precluded by his wounds from making a living, was killed in battle or on a campaign, his family was also looked after, once again by the canton or the community.[54]

The Swiss were a pious people. While on military service, priests accompanied the army to look after their spiritual needs. The priests were always present to say mass, console the wounded, absolve the sinner, administer last rites, and to perform other sacred duties. Before battle, the Confederates customarily knelt in prayer and took mass whenever possible. Frequently, the priests assured them that God and the Holy Virgin would protect them and give them victory. Before the troops rose from their knees, their officers would throw a handful of dirt over them as a reminder that the Swiss return victors or die in the attempt. Frequently, there was no other choice for the troops because they knew that retreat or surrender were usually unthinkable.[55]

Swiss Military Rules

The Swiss system of government was highly important in the making of military policies and rules during the late Middle Ages. The central governing body of the Swiss Confederation was the Federal Diet or *Tagsatzung* (meet for a day). The Federal Diet met at regular intervals, usually three times a year, at one of the major cities in the Confederation. The usual meeting places rotated between Lucerne, Bern, and Zürich. Each state or canton had one vote in the Diet, and the voting had to be unanimous for a resolution to pass, but the enacting of a law by the *Tagsatzung* meant little by itself since the Diet had no power to enforce the measures it passed. Its actual function seems to have been that of making suggestions, primarily on matters of foreign affairs. The implementation of the acts passed by the Diet was left to the individual cantons which was where the real seat of power rested.

The Swiss cantons were very diverse in their political structures. The greatest disparity in political ideologies was between the predominantly urban cantons and the rural cantons. Lucerne, Bern, and Zürich were the primary city-dominated cantons at the close of the fifteenth century, and Uri, Schwyz, and Unterwalden (Obwalden and Nidwalden combined), known collectively as the Forest Cantons, were the principal rustic cantons. Many of the other cantons were various combinations of towns, farms, and pastoral areas. The governments of the Swiss cantons varied from the near aristocratic rule of the city-dominated cantons, most notably Bern, to the near pure democracies of the Forest Cantons. The individual cantons had

---

54 Elgger, *Kriegswesen*, p.171.
55 Elgger, *Kriegswesen*, p.239 and p.424.

the power to enact and enforce their own laws, and the laws carried out in one canton were not necessarily in place in others.[56]

Military rules came primarily from formal legislation or laws and from traditional practices, while custom appears to have been the most influential. The cantons and the Federal Diet often tried to regulate military policy and were usually quite successful. Yet the forms that developed from military necessity over the years, and how problems were resolved by the leaders and troops in the field, meant that innovation as well as established customs and practices proved to be important in military operations.

There were six circumstances under which the Swiss could be called to fight: when a technical state of war existed, when there was reason to fear an attack by an enemy, when fighting had occurred, when there was an agreement to help a foreign state, when hired as mercenaries, and when it was necessary to guard fortresses or to man watch posts. The Swiss Militia, always prepared for war, was an institution able to meet all calls to arms promptly. This war preparedness helped the Confederates be successful in resisting invasion.[57]

After the Battle of Sempach in 1386, the Swiss Federal Diet issued general orders defining acceptable Swiss military conduct. This Sempacher Letter of 1393 set down rules by which the Confederates made war throughout the fifteenth century and beyond. Other suggestions and orders were given at various times, but the Sempacher Letter remained the guiding principle. In this directive, flight was strictly forbidden. If anyone fled, or called for the army to retire, the soldiers next to him were obliged to kill the offender on the spot. Men were often placed at the rear of the army to cut down anyone attempting to flee. Special protection was always given to women, children, and churches. No prisoners could be taken while fighting continued, because it was much easier to kill a man than to hold him, and the encumbrance of captives meant that the successful pursuit of a defeated enemy was less likely.[58]

There were also numerous rules governing the sharing of booty and the amount of plunder which could be brought home. Pillaging was only permissible with the consent of the leaders, and such activity was totally forbidden during battle. Booty was declared common property and was to be distributed as the leaders directed. Punishments were prescribed for the soldier who brought home too much loot or did not correctly share what he took with other men. Laws against soldiers returning with too many spoils came from the fear that foreign influences were corrupting the people and ruining morality.[59]

---

56 John Martin Vincent, *Switzerland at the Beginning of the Sixteenth Century* (Baltimore: the Johns Hopkins Press, 1904), pp.7–10.
57 Elgger, *Kriegswesen*, p.42 and Häne, 'Kriegsbereitschaft,' p.33.
58 *Sempacher Brief* in Frey, *Kriegstaten*, pp.125–7 and Elgger, *Kriegswesen*, pp.214–16.
59 Elgger, *Kriegswesen*, p.80 and Vincent, *Switzerland*, pp.24–9.

SWISS WEAPONS AND ARMOUR

The Swiss were also forbidden from the employ of certain states and peoples to avoid the risk of them fighting against other Confederates or supporting states or causes unfriendly to the Swiss Confederation. In 1500, against the advice of their leaders, Swiss mercenaries were employed by both Luigi Sforza, Duke of Milan, and Louis XII, King of France. When the two armies of Milan and France faced each other the Confederates refused to fight their countrymen, and the Swiss under Sforza returned home.[60]

Cowards and traitors were both despised. Deserters were supposed to be sentenced to death, although there are no known examples of formal executions of tried offenders. Often, their names were recorded to shame them for generations to come. Traitors, especially those who served the much-feared Habsburgs, were the most hated of all men. Great value was placed on the virtues of keeping promises and in being loyal. Frequently

The Second Flemish Rebellion. Woodcut based on a drawing by Hans Springinklee showing the nature of close quarters infantry combat of the period. (Metropolitan Museum of Art, Harris Brisbane Dick Fund, 1928)

---

60   Elgger, *Kriegswesen,* pp.78–9 and Robert Laffont, *The Ancient Art of Warfare* (Paris: Robert Laffont, 1966), vol. 1, p.460.

when the Swiss were hired to fight for other states, they considered themselves allies as much as mercenaries. They thought such loyalties as being part of their responsibilities to their employers, but not at the expense of fighting other Confederates.[61]

---

61   Elgger, *Kriegswesen*, pp.236–7.

2

The Swiss at War

Swiss 'Brutality' and the Treatment of Prisoners

Eminent modern military historians, including Charles Oman and Hans Delbrück, have called the Swiss very brutal soldiers who always killed their prisoners.[1] Such blanket assertions are overly simplistic, misleading, and untrue, and the question of Swiss brutality remains one of the most misunderstood topics of how the Confederates made war. The topic has many aspects, but it focuses on how the Swiss treated people and property when a battle was not in progress. Much of the misunderstanding comes from the general order from the Swiss Federal Diet on 11 March 1499, when it called for all the citizens of the various cantons to take an oath that, when they went to war, no prisoners were to be taken but everyone would be killed, 'as our pious ancestors have always been accustomed' to doing.[2] This order was clearly meant to urge the Swiss to fight hard, but it was largely ignored during the Swabian War.

The Swiss could indeed be brutal as was demonstrated forcefully by the slaughter following the Battle of Calven in 1499 and activities at other times (as will be described below). For example, a group of Confederates stabbed to death two 'handsome' boys, brothers named Wasman, in Habsheim in Alsace, claiming that the children were notoriously misbehaved.[3]

On the other hand, the Swiss could be generous and even merciful to their enemies. A raiding party captured the village of Guttendingen in 1499 and was preparing to burn it when a plea from the poor women, widows, and orphans of the town reached the Confederate leaders, and they spared

---

1   Oman, *Art of War*, vol. 2, pp.253–254 and Delbrück, *Kriegskunst*, vol. 3, p.688.
2   Vincent, *Switzerland*, p.54.
3   'Freiburger Chronik des Schwabenkrieges' in *Aktenstücke*, p.603.

the village.⁴ On another occasion, a Swiss contingent on a raid came to the town of Torenbüren and demanded 2,200 gulden (gold coins) as a ransom for 160 prisoners who had recently been taken. If they were not promptly paid, the Confederates threatened to burn the forest at Bregenz. The Swiss received the money but were so moved by the plight of the poor people in the area that they returned 800 gulden to them, a large sum of money.⁵ Such stories are numerous. The most common acts of generosity shown by the Swiss were the releasing of captured prisoners unharmed and the returning of cattle and foodstuffs to the needy.

The Swiss frequently took prisoners of war during successful raids. Often they took captives when their enemy were surprised in the castles and towns, but more often they simply surrendered to the Swiss. The Confederates would spare a garrison if it surrendered, but if it offered resistance, and the Swiss succeeded in taking the castle or fortress, then the all the defenders could be killed or mistreated at the discretion of the attackers. Usually, in negotiating the surrender of a town or castle, the Swiss would offer a simple ultimatum, surrender or die. Faced with such a choice the garrison usually capitulated. On one occasion, the leader of a garrison put the question of surrender to a vote of the 25 defenders of the castle – 21 voted to surrender, and only 4 wanted to fight, so the castle capitulated.⁶

There were three basic categories of prisoner, defined by social class, taken in the Swabian War – these were prisoners of the nobility, army, and peasantry. The Swiss commonly released the peasantry and other low-class persons after only a brief captivity if they would swear to never again make war on the Confederates. The Swiss considered enemy prisoners from the lower classes to be troublesome if they were to be held in confinement until the end of the war, and they were often released to save cost. Those prisoners were divided up among the contingents that captured them. Captives were usually sent to areas well away from the borders for safekeeping. These men were usually treated well and given adequate food and housing. The treatment of prisoners must have been good because there were only two reported deaths in captivity during the entire Swabian War.⁷

The Swiss gave the nobility special treatment because they were held for ransom, and care was taken to assure that they did not escape. The captives from the upper classes were well treated and spent much of their time

---

4   'Freiburger Chronik des Schwabenkrieges,' in *Aktenstücke*, pp.573–574.
5   Brennwald, *Schweizerchronik*, vol. 2, p.372.
6   Heinrich Hug, *Villinger Chronik von 1495 bis 1533* (Tübingen: Literarischer Verein Stuttgart, 1883), pp.8–9.
7   Burgermeister und Rat zur Chur an Hauptleute, Fähnrich Räte von Chur, Jetzt im Feld, 16 February 1499 in C. and F. Jecklin, *Der Anteil Graubündens am Schwabenkrieg* (Davos: E. Ricter'sche Buchdruckerei, 1899), pp.108–109. See also, Brennwald, *Schweizerchronik*, vol. 2, pp.434 and 438; and Otto Feger, 'Probleme der Kriegsgefangenschaft im Schwabenkrieg,' *Zeitschrift für Schweizerishche Geschichte* (1950), vol. 30, p.597.

writing letters for the required sums of money and in awaiting the delivery of these payments. Young girls carried the money and messages, and were allowed to travel freely between the armies. In 1499, a doctor from Basel helped three captive nobleman's sons escape from Swiss confinement, the boys successfully achieved their freedom, but the doctor was captured and executed as a traitor or criminal.[8]

The late Middle Ages was a period of brutal warfare when soldiers of all nations showed little respect for the lives of others and for private property. The Swiss military was indeed a creature of its age and should be regarded as such. But, it is incorrect to brand the Swiss as showing excessive brutality or cruelty either to people or to their property.

Cavalry of the Swabian League. (Editor's collection)

---

8   Feger, 'Kriegsgefangenschaft,' pp.600–601 and Lenz, *Schwabenkrieg*, pp.87–96.

3

Background and Causes of the Swabian War

Swiss and German Relations

After the Swiss Confederation was first formed in the late thirteenth century, it was immediately at odds with the Habsburg family, who wanted to increase their authority over those areas from which the Swiss were continually gaining new states and allies. During the fourteenth century and the early years of the fifteenth century, the Habsburgs fought many wars with the members of the Confederation over conflicting interests and disputed lands. The Swiss were successful in all of these conflicts. The Habsburgs long remembered the humiliation of being repeatedly defeated by the Swiss peasants, and the Confederates continually feared that Habsburg power was a menace that had never been entirely removed.[1]

For most of the fifteenth century, a member of the Habsburg family also served as the Holy Roman Emperor. The Habsburg, Frederick III, was Emperor from 1439 to 1493, and the Confederate mistrust of the Austrian ruling family naturally became synonymous with the policies of the Holy Roman Empire. By 1499, Swiss participation in Imperial affairs had been voluntary for generations. The origins of Swiss independence can be traced as far back as the Charter of Liberty or *Freibrief* issued by Frederick II, an Emperor of the Hohenstaufen dynasty, to Schwyz in 1240. This was two years before the sealing of Schwyz, Uri, and Unterwalden into their first known pact, and a generation before closer alliances were created later in the century.[2] The Swiss cantons had infrequently participated in the affairs of the Holy Roman Empire, but by the end of the fifteenth century all

---

1 Lenz, *Schwabenkrieg*, p.36.
2 Sidler, *Morgarten*, pp.42–43.

BACKGROUND AND CAUSES OF THE SWABIAN WAR

The Emperor Maximilian, r.1508-1519 . (Metropolitan Museum of Art, Gift of Felix M. Warburg, 1920)

the members of the Confederation except Bern had largely severed their participation in The Empire and had ceased attending the Imperial Diet or legislative body.

Most of the members of the Confederation were on good terms with France late in the fifteenth century, but again Bern was the exception. Bern was the most territorially ambitious canton, and was covetous of the French-speaking areas immediately to its west. It had gained authority over a small number of these areas after the Burgundian Wars (1474–1477) and wanted to acquire more. Bern saw France as its chief opponent in obtaining these areas, and it considered The Empire, France's rival, as its chief potential ally in forwarding its ambitions. As a result, Bern continued participation in the affairs of The Empire, while the other Swiss cantons did little to nothing.

By the end of the fifteenth century, the Habsburgs were beset with problems. The Turks frequently ravaged Habsburg lands in Eastern Europe, a feud continued between the Habsburgs and the Hungarian monarchy, and Bavaria was becoming increasingly hostile to The Empire and to the ruling family of Austria. Clearly, the solutions to these problems could most readily be achieved through the application of military force, but the Habsburgs did not control a good military capable of overcoming all the difficulties facing them. The Habsburgs recognised that the excellent Swiss military could potentially aid them a great deal in these struggles. They further believed that the Confederates would be most effective when employed against the Turks, and for this purpose, they made attempts to gain Swiss friendship and support.[3]

An accord with the Confederates appeared to be a good idea for the Habsburgs, but such an attempt was very unlikely to succeed. The ageing Frederick III was a major hindrance to any such effort since he was openly disdainful of the Swiss Confederation, and his contempt for the Confederates themselves was often interpreted by them as a manifestation of a continuing policy of hostility. Although there had not been a war between the Habsburgs and Swiss since the middle of the fifteenth century, the Confederates continued a tradition of hatred for the ruling house of Austria. This animosity ran so deep that anyone who displayed the emblem of the Habsburgs (the Imperial Eagle) within the Confederation did so at the peril of his life.

Nonetheless, Sigismund, the Emperor Frederick's brother, achieved a brief success in getting Swiss support. In 1474, Sigismund sought an alliance with the Swiss. Because the Confederation was at war with Burgundy at the time, the Confederates found a defensive pact proposed by Sigismund to be desirable. The Eternal Direction of 1474 was designed to assure mutual aid against any threat to the Confederation or to the Habsburgs, whether that menace came from external enemies or disloyal areas within the Holy Roman Empire. Yet the agreement did not last long, because the final defeat of Burgundy in 1477 removed the immediate threat to Swiss security, and Frederick himself, in his constant contempt for the Confederates, refused to negotiate a renewal of the pact.[4]

Problems continued to beset the Holy Roman Empire and the Habsburg family in the 1480s. Since 1477, the Emperor Frederick III had been at war with Hungary, and the war went badly for the Holy Roman Emperor. His forces were driven out of some Austrian areas, and the Hungarians captured Vienna in 1483. Frederick never saw the city again. The Turks' ravages were a continuing menace, and the Bavarians were threatening

---

3   Lenz, *Schwabenkrieg*, p.14.
4   Emil Dürr, 'Die Politik der Eidgenossen im XIV und XV Jahrhundert,' *Schweizer Kriegsgeschichte* (1933), vol. 4, pp.463–465.

Habsburg power in South Germany. Additionally, Sigismund, who was Erzherzog (Archduke) of Austria and Frederick's distant cousin, tried to take the Tyrol, in the western part of Austria, away from the Emperor's control in 1487.[5] Some decisive action needed to be taken to strengthen the royal family's interests, and Maximilian, Frederick's son and heir, was highly effective in helping the situation.

The Creation of the Swabian Infantry

Maximilian (1459–1519) was a young, energetic leader in the 1480s years before he was elected to his father's throne. His position within The Empire became increasingly important as he matured because of the ageing of Frederick, who had once been a powerful ruler but became more feeble with age. To help alleviate the ruling family's problems, Maximilian began a programme of reorganising The Empire's army in the mid–1480s. He realised that the Swiss infantry's organisation and tactics could be copied, and starting in 1485, he went to the Swabian areas of South Germany and began to organise its manpower along Confederate lines.[6]

The heir to the throne of Austria recognised that a military force based on a peasant infantry was potentially loyal to a central monarch and could be more useful than the noble cavalry because the men from the lower classes could more easily be controlled. Maximilian also realised that, as the Swiss had proven, a good infantry could be very effective in battle. Naturally, the most valuable persons needed to help train the Swabians along Swiss lines were the Confederates themselves. An obscure knight, Konrad Gächuf von Kesswil, was the most instrumental person in hiring Swiss mercenaries to teach the Swabians Confederate organisation, tactics, et cetera and the use of their weaponry.[7] Gächuf's activities were potentially dangerous for the Swiss, and the Federal Diet soon called him into account. He was accused of 'wanting to arm and instruct the Swabians and other Landsknechts so that one of them would be worth more than two Confederates' on the field of battle.[8]

From 1486, when Gächuf's Swiss began their instruction, the Swabian infantry began to prove its abilities on the battlefields of Europe. These Swabian infantry, the Landsknechts, had a deep hatred for the Swiss, who shared the Swabian southern border. This hostility stemmed from feuds leading to raids and petty intermittent warfare between those two peoples going back many generations. The Swabian infantry, with high morale and confidence obtained from their victories on the battlefields of Europe,

---

5 Dürr, 'Politik,' pp.469–470.
6 Dürr, 'Politik,' p.466; Frey, *Kriegstaten*, p.335.
7 Häne, 'Kriegsbereitschaft,' pp.11–12.
8 *Amtliche Sammlung der ältern Eidgenössischen Abschiede.* 8 vols. (Lucerne: Wener'sche Buchdruckerei, 1858–1874), vol. 3, p.250.

THE SWABIAN WAR OF 1499

Herald of the Swabian League. His cap, tabard and hose are black and yellow, the arms on the shield are lions or on a field gules. (Editor's collection)

soon showed their contempt for the Swiss and became anxious to test their abilities against their former teachers and mentors.[9]

To assure the use of the Swabian infantry and to form a political power base capable of aiding the Habsburgs and their problems, Maximilian and Frederick formed the Swabian League in February 1488, consisting of the knights and cities in the area. The Swabian League, with the Swabian infantry, or Landsknechts, as its primary military contingent, was successful in aiding Maximilian in retaining Bavaria and in defeating the rebellious Sigismund to keep control of the Tyrol.[10]

The existence of the powerful Swabian League on their borders made the Swiss suspicious of its intended purposes. Even though the League was apparently aimed primarily at Bavaria, the Confederates feared that Frederick would one day be tempted to use the League against them. The south German nobility in the Swabian League did nothing to help calm such fears. The German Lords were contemptuous of the Confederation; as they watched their feudal rights weaken from the pressures of a discontented peasantry prone to violence, these nobles became fearful that the existence of the free and often democratic Swiss Confederation on their borders was a serious social threat because their peasants were seeking freedoms similar to those enjoyed by many Confederates. As a result, there was much talk among the German nobility of dividing up the Confederation, repressing Swiss liberties, and establishing noble rule over them.[11] The Confederates, long protective of their hard-won rights, hated any idea of having a German nobility established in their lands and seeing their privileges restricted or abolished.[12] The agitation from such talk and the mutual hatred between the Swiss and the Swabians almost broke into war in October 1488, but before there was any clash of arms, angers cooled, and war was averted for a time.[13]

---

9   Peterman Etterlin. *Kronica von der loblichen Eidgnoschaft* (Basel: Eckenstein, 1752), p.231 and Dürr, 'Politik,' p.474.
10 Dürr, 'Politik,' p.470.
11 Christopher Hare, *Maximilian the Dreamer: Holy Roman Emperor, 1459–1519* (New York: Charles Scribner's Sons, 1913), p.98.
12 Lenz, *Schwabenkrieg*, p.27.
13 Frey, *Kriegstaten*, p.334.

The Kings of France had long waged an unfriendly policy against the Holy Roman Empire, believing their best interests were served by undermining the strength of The Empire. France's policy included retaining good terms with the Confederates to assure the availability of Swiss mercenaries, and to influence the Confederation to remain on unfavourable terms with The Empire. The agents of King Charles VIII of France (1470–1498) were active in the Confederation, distributing funds and anti-Imperial propaganda. Charles further stirred up Swiss feelings by employing mercenaries from the Swiss cantons which bordered Swabia, where the Confederates were already most antagonistic towards the Swabians, and these mercenaries were used against The Empire and the Swabian infantry on operations in Flanders.[14]

French influence over the Confederation was demonstrated when, in 1486, 3,000 Swiss mercenaries in the service of The Empire in Flanders left Maximilian's Army and joined the French Army. This, and other similar actions in the following years, convinced many German nobles and many Swabian infantry alike that the Swiss were disloyal to The Empire and could not be trusted. With mutual Swiss and Swabian hatred intensifying, France enjoyed increasing diplomatic success. In 1491, King Charles concluded a five-year peace and neutrality pact with eight cantons of the Confederation as a gesture of mutual friendship and support. The Swiss cantons were happy to sign the agreement because the pact assured the continued flow of French funds into their lands, and because it assured French support in case of war.

Maximilian's Attempts at Unity

Long before the death of his father on 19 August 1493, Maximilian had sought reforms that would unify and strengthen The Empire.[15] The Habsburg noble sought to exert more control over the Holy Roman Empire by instituting the Common Penny (*Gemeiner Pfennig*) or universal tax and by strengthening the Imperial Supreme Court. The Common Penny was designed to be paid by all the members of The Empire. Maximilian wanted to use the funds he received from this tax to support a military that would protect The Empire, and Habsburg interests, from external enemies and to assure the loyalty of the various areas within The Empire. The Supreme Court was intended to handle all legal affairs within The Empire to guarantee justice and peace. Maximilian explained his reforms at the Diet at Worms in 1495. He promised the various lands of The Empire a voice in the government if the Common Penny was paid. He also spoke

---

14 Dürr, 'Politik,' pp.481–482.
15 Frey, *Kriegstaten*, p.334.

of re-establishing the ancient boundaries of The Empire, which were in fact largely indefinable, and he fervently warned of the danger of disunity.[16]

Despite Maximilian's intense plea for unity, the political adjustments were not well received by many members of the Diet, and the Swiss believed that the reforms simply did not apply to them. Most of the Swiss cantons had not been involved in Imperial affairs for decades, and only representatives from Bern were present at the Diet in Worms in 1495. The other cantons were unwilling to consider these reforms as anything more than vain rhetoric. They believed that the Common Penny was unnecessary for them, because they already had a fine military system, and the Supreme Court of the Empire was in direct conflict with their own developing system of laws and courts known as the Justice Awakening. In short, the Swiss Confederation was progressing towards its own distinct national character and was sure to resent any attempt by The Empire to hamper or limit that development.[17] When Maximilian's representatives visited the Confederation to institute the Common Penny, they were politely yet definitely turned away in most areas – Zürich's City Council refused even to see the emissaries.[18]

The Supreme Court of the Empire soon handed down unfavourable judgements regarding certain lands controlled by the Swiss allies of Rottweil and Schaffhausen. The Court stated that the two towns did not legally own the territories in question, and these should be turned over to The Empire. Rottweil and Schaffhausen, supported by the Confederation, refused to vacate the disputed areas, thus choosing to ignore the judgement of the Supreme Court. Angered by Swiss defiance, Maximilian threatened to go to war if the Swiss refused to relent. The Confederation would not be bullied; rather, the Swiss cantons began to prepare for war. To make good on his threat, Maximilian also began preparations for war. Even though negotiations continued, both sides were clearly disinterested in compromising.[19]

The Empire's war preparations advanced slowly, but much of the Confederation was soon on a war footing. As a precautionary measure, from 1490 the Swiss cities began to store a year's supply of grain and, in 1495, the Confederates restricted grain exports through the St Gotthard Pass. During the crisis of 1488, which nearly ended in war, Swiss representatives from the various cantons had met in Zürich to assure unity of action should the dangerous situation result in an armed conflict with The Empire. At this conference, Zürich, Bern, Lucerne, Uri, Schwyz, Unterwalden, Zug, Glarus, Fribourg, and Solothurn pledged mutual support in defence of each other. Other areas of the Confederation, Apenzell, St Gallen, and Wallis were not represented, but the agreement clearly included them. A

---

16 Dürr, 'Politik,' pp.481–482.
17 Dürr, 'Politik,' pp.484–485.
18 Frey, *Kriegstaten*, p.336.
19 Frey, *Kriegstaten*, p.338.

BACKGROUND AND CAUSES OF THE SWABIAN WAR

Storming of Moran, by Hans Burgkmair, completed 1515–1516. The print is notable for depicting artillery, infantry and cavalry working together in cooperation. (Metropolitan Museum of Art, Rogers Fund 1918)

decade later, as talk of war progressed, all of these areas were willing to honour this pledge. Only Bern spoke of peace, but this canton clearly felt a much greater allegiance to the Confederation than to The Empire.[20]

As the Swiss Confederation and the Holy Roman Empire moved closer to war, another dispute became heated between members of the Grey Leagues (Graubünden or Grisons) and the Austrian Tyrol. The Grey Leagues bordered the Confederation on the east, and they consisted of areas around Chur, called the Rätier. The Grey Leagues was a small alliance of three tiny states similar to the Swiss Confederation. The people of the Rätier had formed an agreement in 1424 to ensure their independence from the

---

20 Häne, 'Kriegsbereitschaft,' pp.20–22; Brennwald, *Schweizerchronik*, vol. 2, p.339; and Frey, *Kriegstaten*, p.339.

Habsburgs, but by the end of the century, the threat from the ruling family of Austria made this self-rule uncertain. The Habsburgs controlled the Tyrol, which bordered the Grey Leagues, and the two areas became involved in boundary disputes because their borders had never been clearly defined. Free peasants, and those owing allegiance to the Bishop of the Tyrol, lived in these disputed areas, often in the same communities. The Grey Leagues asked that all these locations be made free presumably to join their alliance, but the regency of the Tyrol was unwilling to hear anything about these extended privileges. The leaders of the Tyrol believed it was preferable to go to war rather than give the disputed areas the independence that would allow them to join the Grey League.[21]

The Habsburg authority in Innsbruck began to pressure the Grey Leagues, which realised they did not have the strength to test the power of the Tyrol alone, so that the alliance turned to the Swiss Confederation for help since the two coalitions had long enjoyed good relations. The similar culture, society, and beliefs in freedom and independence shared by the two coalitions helped them form a bond of friendship to face the mounting threat from the Habsburgs. Much to the anger of the Habsburgs, the Grey Leagues joined a close agreement with the Confederation in June 1497. Another two small pacts, the League of God's House (*Gotteshausbund*), and the Ten Jurisdictions (*Zehngerichtebund*), both near the Grey Leagues, also felt endangered by the Tyrol and, in 1498, also joined in a close accord with the Confederation. These areas proved to be valuable allies and fought with the Confederation in the Swabian War.[22]

The Swiss made some final attempts at negotiation by sending emissaries to the Federal Diet asking to be free of the Common Penny and the Supreme Court of the Empire. Their requests were rejected.[23] In the spring of 1497, a number of Swiss emissaries met with the Archbishop and Elector of Mainz, Bertold von Hennenberg (1442–1504). The church leader explained that the Confederate representatives must be obedient to The Empire and accept the reforms on taxation, the courts, and the army that had been recently proposed. To all this, the Swiss gave mild answers, saying they had no authority to act and would relay the messages to their leaders. In an obvious attempt to bully the Confederates, Archbishop Bertold told them they needed to be under a noble, or nobles, and thus Imperial suzerainty, and he showed them a goose feather pen with which he could easily sign the appropriate papers to place the Confederation under a church interdict. According to the contemporary Swiss chronicler, Heinrich Brennwald, one of the Confederates, speaking on his own volition, retorted that weapons had been sent to subjugate the Swiss which they could fear, but they were not afraid of goose feathers. Another contemporary account of this same

---

21   Frey, *Kriegstaten*, pp.339–340 and Fritz Rieter, 'Der Schwabenkrieg vor 450 Jahren,' *Schweizer Monatshefte* (June 1949) vol. 29, p.132.
22   Elgger, *Kriegswesen*, p.398.
23   Elgger, *Kriegswesen*, p.398.

incident reported that the man was laughing and said that a conquest by the signing of a document, 'was doubtful, since it had often been tried with pikes, halberds, and cannon but that had not yet been achieved.'[24] The negotiations having failed, war almost became inevitable. All that was needed were some minor incidents to start hostilities.

To weaken the Swiss position, The Empire attempted to strip the Confederation of all the areas which owed them allegiance. Isprugg, an independent town far from the other Swiss cantons, was offered spiritual salvation to desert the Swiss and join the Swabian League. The offer was for salvation, but the implication was clear that if Isprugg did not willingly desert the Confederation, it would face the Swabian League as an enemy. Isolated from the Confederation and weak, Isprugg had no choice but to comply. Mulhouse (Mülhausen), caught in a similar situation, also complied with the Habsburg demands. The city of Constance had long been friendly to the Swiss but because of Habsburg pressure turned to The Empire and was lost to the Swiss Confederation. That situation proved to be a serious blow to the Confederates because Constance became one of the major garrison points of the Imperial Army during the Swabian War.[25]

---

24 Brennwald, *Schweizerchronik*, vol. 2, p.334; Anshelm, *Berner-Chronik*, vol. 2, p.112.
25 Brennwald, *Schweizerchronik*, vol. 2, p.334; Frey, *Kriegstaten*, p.339.

4

The Swabian War

Hostilities Begin

In the winter of 1498–1499, forces from both sides were stationed along the border between the Swiss and Habsburg lands with the opposing troops watching and waiting to see if the other would make a move. The River Rhine formed the boundary between Swiss and Imperial lands in many places, including in the headwaters of the stream in the areas near modern Liechtenstein. The hatred and sense of rivalry between the armies on both sides did not long remain dormant. The Swiss made the first martial moves when they seized mountain passes in the Alps and Jura mountains, but because they met no resistance, the actual fighting did not start with these actions.[1] Late in January 1499 soldiers from the Tyrol crossed the Rhine into the Grey Leagues although with no known objective. They were quickly confronted and driven back across the River, and with this act, the Grey Leagues were at war with the Tyrol.[2]

The entire Swiss Confederation was not automatically at war at that point, although the members would soon feel obligated to come to the aid of their newly-acquired ally. However, a border incident soon brought the entire Confederation into the conflict. The troops of the Swabian League and the Swiss Confederation faced each other in a tense situation along the Rhine. Feeling the traditional hatred between the two peoples and bored by occupying static positions in the cold, winter months, the two armies amused themselves by shouting insults back and forth. At the Castle of Gutenberg, near Balzers in modern Liechtenstein, the Swabian infantry

---

1 Hans Ungelter an Esslingen, 1 February 1499 in K. Klüpfel, (ed.) *Urkunden zur Geschichte des Schwäbischen Bundes (1488–1533)* (Stuttgart: Literarischer Verein, 1846), vol. 1, p.281.
2 Frey, *Kriegstaten*, p.341.

THE SWABIAN WAR

The Swabian War. The areas of operation

THE SWABIAN WAR OF 1499

mocked the Swiss by composing unchristian songs that were insulting to the pious Confederates. The final provocation came when the Swabian troops displayed a cow and called to the Swiss to come over to make love to it and to act as the animal's groom. Then to complete the insult, the Swabians mooed like cows. The Swiss were infuriated at the obvious implications and suggestion. In retaliation, the Swiss leader from Uri, Heinrich Wolleb, took a group of men across the Rhine on 6 February 1499 and burnt a house and a stall. At this point, the war thus began in earnest.[3]

At the war's beginning, the forces on both sides were quickly aligned. The Lower Union of cities on the Rhine fought for The Empire. Of their number only Basel, which had greater economic ties with the Swiss Confederation, was able to remain neutral.[4] The only other important city that managed to stay neutral was Rottweil.[5] The Empire called for support from all its lands, but it was the Tyrol and the Swabian League that contributed most of the support. The Swiss Confederation called upon its members and on its allies including the Grey Leagues and France.[6] Even though the five-year peace and neutrality pact between France and the Confederation had expired

The Battle of Marignano (13–14 September 1515), Urs Graf. Although 15 years after the Battle of Dornach, both battles would have looked similar given the troops involved on both sides of the fighting. Graf, from Switzerland, had military experience and is believed to have fought at Marignano. (Wikimedia commons)

---

3   Frey, *Kriegstaten*, p.342.
4   Luginbühl, 'Bruderholz,' p.205.
5   Dürr, 'Politik,' p.503.
6   Rieter, 'Schwabenkrieg,' p.134.

in 1496, the new king, Louis XII (1462–1515), had pledged French aid in the event of war; this assistance was supposed to be in the form of money and artillery. The funds reached the Confederation, but the cannon were delayed in Burgundy, and did not arrive until the war was over. Except for French money, the Swiss Confederation and the Grey Leagues had to fight the war with minimal outside help.

5

Fighting a Costly War

War Strategy

The Swabian War, often called the Swiss War (*Schweizerkrieg*) in Germany, was poorly planned by both sides. Overall strategy consisted largely of border raids which entailed the destruction of villages and castles and the taking of cattle and loot. The eminent historian of Swiss military history, Hans Rudolf Kurz, has described the conflict as war for war's sake, which also included a number of bitter battles in which neither belligerent employed its whole army.[1]

The Empire had to wait many weeks before enough troops mustered to take definitive action. The initial Imperial strategic plan was to assemble troops at various locations around castles, fortified towns, and to construct defences of various types. From these bases, the army was to resist Confederate attacks and then raid into Swiss territories at the most favourable opportunities. The command of those operations was divided between Heinrich von Fürstenberg and his two brothers, Wolfgang and Ulrich.[2] In April 1499, Maximilian himself came to South Germany to give the war more definitive direction, and he decided to fight against the Grey Leagues first. After two disastrous defeats at the Battle of Frastanz and the Battle of Calven in April and May 1499 respectively, and following a difficult and indecisive mountain campaign in June, Maximilian turned his attention directly to the Swiss Confederation. When the Swiss defeated Heinrich von Fürstenberg at the Battle of Dornach in July, the fighting

---

1 Kurz, *Schweizerschlachten*, p.141.
2 'Kriegsplan des Schwäbischen Bundes gegen die Eidgenossenschaft,' 20 January 1499 in *Aktenstücke*, pp.3–4.

FIGHTING A COSTLY WAR

quickly died down, and the belligerents signed a peace treaty at Basel on 22 September 1499.[3]

Major problems beset Maximilian in waging the war. He had insufficient funds to pay his troops, and contingents of his army from various parts of The Empire were continually squabbling over petty matters, making a unified war effort challenging. The Emperor tried to bring some unity and direction to his army and war effort by personally overseeing the war preparations. He rose before everyone else in the morning and worked well into the night. He spoke only about the war and was continually trying to get more funds while writing many letters to that end, but his finances were always inadequate.[4]

The Battle Near Hulst, by Hans Burgkmair, completed 1515–1516. The engraving shows the chaotic and close nature of infantry warfare in the late fifteenth and early sixteenth centuries. (Metropolitan Museum of Art, Rogers Fund 1918)

---

3   Kurz, *Schweizerschlachten*, pp.144–145.
4   'Augustin Somenza an den Herzog von Mailand,' 19 April 1499 in

The overall Swiss strategy did not differ greatly from that of The Empire. The Confederates had garrisons at various castles and fortified towns and churches near their borders to meet the enemy when possible and to use as staging areas to raid into enemy territory. Swiss funds to pay their troops were often lacking, but numerous successful excursions and raids frequently provided enough booty to pay many soldiers. Major offensives into enemy territory were impractical because two-thirds of the Swiss border faced The Empire, and it took a great many men just to watch the borders.[5]

The Swiss Confederation had yet to achieve strong political solidarity, and the Alliance went to war without the enthusiastic support of every canton. Basel had long been on friendly terms with the Confederation, but it was not yet a member, and the city managed to stay technically neutral during the conflict. Its main contribution to the war effort went little beyond, on several occasions, feeding groups of Swiss soldiers.[6] The largest detriment to a unified war effort was Bern's indifference. This City Canton had not wanted to fight The Empire, and it gave reluctant support to the war effort. The Cantons of Bern and Zürich had the largest populations at the time, but Bern was the most powerful state militarily in the Confederation, and its half-hearted war effort meant that the Swiss cantons were fighting at a disadvantage. When Bern's troops marched out of the city early in February 1499, the people lining the streets made fun of the fact that so few men accompanied the city's military banners.[7]

Superior strategy was a small factor in the Swiss successes during the conflict. The Confederates owed much of their achievements to the militia and to war preparedness, to their better information about troop movements, and to their military skill learned from traditions and practices that went back generations. Before the war had begun, Confederate scouts were already reconnoitring The Empire's troop movements and dispositions. These men moved rapidly on horseback over the countryside, gathering and delivering timely information.[8] Swiss determination also showed itself in numerous fights and in many battles and skirmishes. Even their German adversaries were impressed with the Confederate fighting ability and discipline.

Aktenstücke, pp.166–167.
5 Kurz, *Schweizerschlachten*, pp.141–142.
6 Lenz, *Schwabenkrieg*, pp.107–108.
7 'Wilhelm Felga an Freiburg,' 12 February 1499 in *Aktenstücke*, pp.42–44.
8 Elgger, *Kriegswesen*, p.331.

FIGHTING A COSTLY WAR

Although later than the Battle of Dornach, this illustration of a pike division of Landsknechts demonstrates the dense formations the troops fought in, c. 1534, possibly by Erhard Schön. (Rijksmuseum, Amsterdam)

Swiss Discipline at the Rhine Crossing

Early in the war, during the winter of 1499, the Swiss demonstrated strict military conduct and great fortitude under the most trying circumstances as recorded by Willibald Pirckheimer, a German participant in the war. At the time raids were staged across the headwaters of the Rhine before the stream emptied into Lake Constance. Both sides of the conflict were eager for revenge for past raids and incursions, and they used the fact that the flow of the Rhine was relatively low that time of year because the spring runoff had not yet begun to cross the River at various points. A column of Swiss troops was attempting to ford the river when a report reached them from their mounted reconnaissance that there were German and Swabian heavy cavalry nearby and perhaps planning to ambush them. Suspecting a trap by a large army contingent, the Confederate leader ordered his men to stop and wait for developments rather than to push forward. There was no thought of withdrawing before even seeing the enemy, because such an action was considered ignominious.

The Swiss stood, in good order, for two hours in freezing water with ice flows so thick that the men had to push them away with their weapons. The water was so deep that it came up to the shoulders of some and even to the chins of others, but the men did not flinch because they thought it to be a great disgrace to break formation – even under a most trying situation. They stood until they were sure no large body of the enemy was approaching. Some of the Confederates died from exposure, and others lost feet and hands to the cold water, but none of them left the battle formation.[9] It is always impressive when a participant in a war praises his enemy, but aspects of this account may be exaggerated: if the troops had indeed stood in freezing water for two hours, all of them would probably have died. Even so, Pirckheimer's account supports the argument that the Swiss had a strong reputation and were highly disciplined troops.

Devastation and the Tragedy of War

The war was confined mostly to the border areas, and raids and brief expeditions were constant factors in the conflict. Many valleys and regions along the Rhine River were raided several times, bringing devastation to these areas. Burning villages and starving people, driven from their homes as refugees or taken as hostages, were common in both Swiss and German areas. At times, certain territories suffered fighting night and day.[10] The nature of the war was so violent that it soon followed its own logic, and successful attacks on the enemy often invited retaliation to avenge the pain and devastation already inflicted on the other.[11] Fighting often occurred at so many places simultaneously that the action became difficult to follow.

The war caused many problems with plague and disease, wolves, and starvation. The plague was a menace whenever bodies were left to the vermin, and it took its toll on many unfortunate victims.[12] Another problem was with wolves. In many areas, the war's dead went unburied, a situation that stemmed from the fact that no one wanted to bury the enemy dead. The area around Constance was notably bad because the opposing armies remained near each other, and fighting was frequent. The bodies were then left to rot or to be devoured by birds, rats, and wolves. The wolves so gorged themselves on human flesh that they developed a taste for it and reputedly began to wander far and wide attacking adults and children. To control the situation in The Empire, orders were given to kill all wolves on sight.[13]

---

9 Pirckheimer, *Schweizerkrieg*, German, pp.130–131.
10 'Hauptleute, Venner et cetera im Feld [Werdenberg] an Zürich,' 28 March 1499 *Aktenstücke*, pp.109–10.
11 'Hans Ungelter an Esslingen,' 10 February 1499 in *Urkunden zur Geschichte des Schwäbischen Bundes*, vol. 1, p.284.
12 'Landeshauptmann an der Etsch und Räte zu Meran an Statthalter und Regenten in Innsbruck,' *Der Anteil Graubündens*, pp.183–4.
13 Martin Crussi, *Schwäbischer Chronik*, Johann Jacob (trans.) (Franckfurt: Metzler und Erhart, 1733), vol. 2, p.152.

A great deal of the war's ferocity came from the bitterness between the combatants. On the borders of the Grey Leagues, both the Swiss and Tyrolean peasants clashed daily, burning and killing. Despair set in among the Tyrolean peasantry because of the great destruction, and they feared that the judgement of God was upon them.[14] Even through the ravages of a brutal war, many Swiss maintained a belief that God was with them. A raiding party of Germans burnt a church in Sennawald, and while the church was entirely burnt to the ground, the Holy Eucharist remained completely untouched and unharmed. Many Confederates took this as a good omen that helped them take courage in difficult times.[15]

The entire war was needless and futile. The conflict could have been avoided, and it solved little. But the military operations were tragic for the peasants both in The Empire and the Confederation who paid a very high price for the war in privations and suffering.

The Battle of Bruderholz, 22 March 1499

One of the first major engagements in the war was the fight at Bruderholz on 22 March 1499, and it proved to be one of the best examples of the Swiss using good mobility and surprise to effectively meet and overwhelm their adversaries. Two days before the engagement, a Swiss detachment of 800 men from Solothurn, Lucerne, and Lenzburg left the area around the village of Dornach near Basel to raid the Sundgau Valley of Alsace. In their absence, an Imperial force of 3,000 infantry and cavalry entered the Birs Valley and began to plunder and burn the villages in the area. They burnt most of the village of Dornach and sent its 10 defenders fleeing to the garrison at the Castle of Dorneck commanded by Benedikt Hugi. This same area was to witness the Battle of Dornach four months later on 22 July 1499.

The 800 Swiss returned as rapidly as possible upon receiving word of the German attack. They arrived early in the morning of 22 March 1499 and spent most of the morning in search of the enemy force. At last, the Confederates received word that the enemy was withdrawing up the Birs Valley towards the Rhine. The Swiss force assembled in battle order and moved into the Bruderholz forest, still maintaining their formation. Just before noon, the Imperial column marched past the Swiss, who were completely unnoticed in their hiding places. The Confederates waited for the signal to attack the enemy in the rear. The German infantry offered no resistance, and they immediately broke and fled. The Imperial cavalry fought a delaying action against the advancing Swiss, hampering any effective pursuit of the fleeing infantry. The cavalry did not remain behind long and soon joined the foot soldiers in flight. The Confederates suffered

---

14 'Hans Ungelter an Esslingen,' 22 February 1499 in *Urkunden zur Geschichte des Schwäbischen Bundes*, vol. 1, pp.293–294.
15 Etterlin, *Kronica*, p.236.

only one fatality, while their adversaries lost 600 or 800 dead according to Swiss sources and as few as 100 from the German records; all the dead were buried in a mass grave. The Germans fled the two miles to the Rhine River and continued their retreat after crossing. Some fled to Basel seeking a place of refuge, but the officials of the city refused to admit them.[16]

The Battle of Schwaderloh (Triboltingen), 11 April 1499

By early April 1499, Maximilian had assembled an impressive army around Constance, these forces coming primarily from Swabia, Austria, and Bavaria. Many of these men had assembled in retaliation for recent Swiss incursions, most notably a campaign in the Hegau Valley east of Schaffhausen. In the last days of March, the Confederates ravaged the Hegau burning the castles of Allisberg, Ranndeck, Roseneck, Frydingen, Stutzlingen, Hamburg, Stouffenn, and Rietheim and destroying the nearby villages.[17]

Facing the German forces at Constance was a series of Confederate garrisons protecting the Thurgau which were manned mostly by men from the region, but they also included detachments from other areas of the Confederation. The village of Ermatingen was garrisoned by 400 men from Bern and Fribourg, and these forces engaged in almost daily skirmishes with detachments from Constance, and the Swiss village of Ow was subject to frequent bombardment from the cannon positioned in the German city. To return fire, Lucerne sent two large cannon early in April. This threat of artillery in Ermatingen prompted Wolfgang von Fürstenberg to lead a major attack on the village to capture the two weapons.[18]

Early in the morning of 11 April 1499, Fürstenberg moved his men by boat on the Rhine and then overland to strike the Swiss garrison at dawn when these men were rousing from sleep. The leader of the Bernese, Hans Kuttler, and the commander of the men from Fribourg, Jacky Henni, were close friends, and they were talking early in the morning before the rest of the men had arisen. An alarm sounded, and the two leaders went to see what was happening only to find the Imperial forces attacking the village from their rear. The Swiss tried to organise some resistance, but the enemy advance was too swift and heavy for the Confederates to get into formation. Some were cut down trying to dress or to arm themselves, and the Master of Artillery (*Büchsenmeister*), Rüdolf Hass from Lucerne, was stabbed to

---

16 Benedikt Hugi an Soloturn 19 and 22 March 1499; and Soloturn an Freiburg 22 March 1499 in *Aktenstücke*, pp.97–99; Lenz, *Schwabenkrieg*, p.80; Anshelm, *Berner-Chronik*, vol. 2, pp.153–154; Rudolf Luginbühl, 'Das Gefecht auf dem Bruderholz,' *Basler Jahrbuch* (1904), p.205.
17 Lenz, *Schwabenkrieg*, p.57 and p.63.
18 Anshelm, *Berner-Chronik*, vol. 2, p.164 and Lenz, *Schwabenkrieg*, p.64.

Swiss plundering the Hegau Valley. (Author's collection)

death. Some of the men from Ermatingen rushed to help the garrison, but the Swabians began shouting, 'Flee, all is lost, alas dear Confederates!' And at that moment, the Swiss broke in flight leaving 73 dead, most of whom were killed while still in bed.[19]

---

19 'Lucerne an Freiburg,' 13 April 1499 in *Aktenstücke*, pp.135–135; Anshelm, *Berner-Chronik*, vol. 2, pp.163–164; and Lenz, *Schwabenkrieg*, p.64.

THE SWABIAN WAR OF 1499

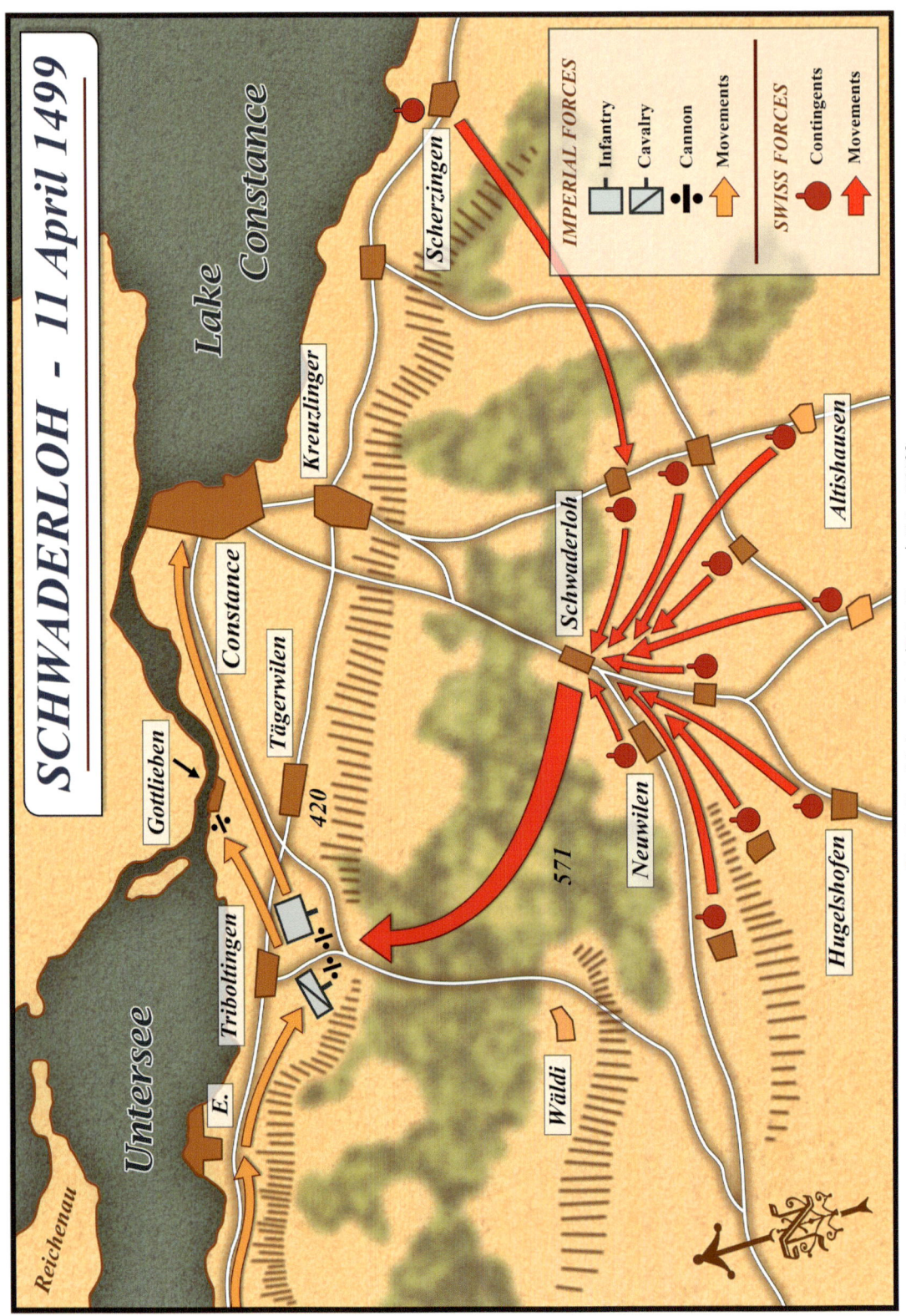

The Battle of Schwaderloh (Triboltingen), 11 April 1499

The Imperial forces soon took Ermatingen, Triboltingen, and Mannenbach. Rushed with success a Swabian leader, Burckhart von Randeck, a noted hater of the Swiss, called for the destruction of the Swiss villages and swore to destroy many enemy areas that day. The Swabians fell out for plunder, and the men from the Hegau began to take their revenge on the Confederates. In Ermatingen some people fled to a church for refuge, but the building was burnt and 37 people killed in it. Many others, including women and children, were killed and the possessions of even small children and sick people were taken. Women, children, and the elderly were abused in various ways, and women and young girls were raped. The three villages were held for three hours before their destruction was complete. On leaving, the Imperial forces filled the houses with straw and set them on fire. Loaded with plunder, the Swabians began the trek back to Constance.[20]

The Swiss garrison fled until they felt safe and then reorganised themselves into order. For the two leaders, the defeat was hard to bear. In their shame and misery, they cried they had lost their manliness. Eager to avenge themselves, they called for the militia to be assembled. Bells rang and fires were lit as signals for the men to assemble at the church in Schwaderloh. The militia soon arrived, and the situation was explained to them in emotional speeches in which the men were warned that they were in danger of losing face for all time. With the contingents from Bern and Fribourg, the total forces now numbered about 1,500. They were all placed into good order under the command of Kuttler and Henni and then marched through a forest on the way to Ermatingen. The Swiss remained in formation despite the thick trees when they received word that their enemies were withdrawing with their loot. Their leaders decided to attack immediately. The Swiss knelt in prayer, rose, and advanced from the forest to meet the Imperial forces near Triboltingen.[21]

The Swabians left two cannon to protect their rear when they retreated, but these artillery pieces were poorly aimed. When the Swiss came out of the forest, the weapons shot too high. The guns were soon taken, but their smoke momentarily obscured the field of battle. Neither force could see the other as the Swiss continued their advance past the cannon to fall upon the Swabians. The Imperial infantry was in two groups and were only interested in escape. The Swiss shouted their battle cry, a Swabian standard bearer broke in flight, and the rest of the infantry followed offering no resistance. Only the heavy cavalry turned to meet the attacking Swiss, but the cavalry's stand was unsuccessful, and the horsemen soon joined the flight.[22]

---

20   Lenz, *Schwabenkrieg*, pp.66–67.
21   Anshelm, *Berner-Chronik* vol. 2, pp.165–166 and Lenz, *Schwabenkrieg*, p.68.
22   'Georg von Emershofen an Nördlingen,' 14 April 1499 in *Urkunden zur Geschichte des Schwäbischen Bundes*, vol. 1, pp.315–317.

The Bernese and men from Fribourg then began to take their revenge for the morning's skirmish. One source reported that at this juncture the action became too confusing to record accurately. The Swabians dropped their plunder, weapons, and flags and fled to their boats. The vessels soon became so full that they overturned and sank, drowning many men. Others died in the river trying to swim across, and many fled all day and throughout the next night. The Swiss pursued, killing any enemy they could overtake, and hunting down and despatching those they found hiding in the forests.[23]

The Confederates reported 1,300 Swabian dead on the field and 80 more bodies fished out of the River Rhine. The Swiss admitted to a loss of 20 men in the battle, including one old man. Soon after the engagement, priests and women, many of them wives of the missing, came to look among the dead for their loved ones. The captured enemy leaders were treated well, and those not held for ransom were sent to Constance after a prisoner exchange had quickly been arranged. Some of the Imperial dead were buried on the field where they had fallen, but most of them were left to rot where they lay and to be devoured by birds and wild animals.[24]

The remarkable feature of this battle was the fact that the members of the militia had no idea they would participate in a major engagement when they awoke that morning. They started the day as they would any other, but within hours they had formed themselves into an army complete with weapons, armour, leaders, and battle formations capable of immediate and effective campaigning. It was no wonder that it was very challenging to attack Swiss territories at this time because an effective military organisation was always on hand on a moment's notice.

Torture and Murder at Tiengen

A Swiss force of 1,500 men from Fribourg, Zürich, Lucerne, and Schaffhausen crossed the Rhine on 18 April 1499 and advanced towards Tiengen (modern Waldshut-Tiengen), but the garrison in the town initially refused to surrender and put up some resistance. Finally, an agreement was reached and the town capitulated. Around 20 to 24 persons were held as prisoners, most of whom were nobles. The remaining garrison, 1,400 soldiers, were forced to strip to their shirts and to take an oath that they would never again make war on the Swiss. These miserable men faced a humiliation and were marched, nearly naked, past the Swiss and then allowed to go home.[25]

---

23 'Freiburger Chronik des Schwabenkrieges' in *Aktenstücke*, p.587.
24 'Graf Wolfgang von Fürstenberg an Herzog Ulrich zu Wirtemberg,' 15 April 1499 in *Aktenstücke*, p.140; Anshelm, *Berner-Chronik*, vol. 2, pp.168–169; Lenz, *Schwabenkrieg*, p.69 and pp.73–74; Brennwald, *Schweizerchronik*, vol. 2, p.402.
25 Anshelm, *Berner-Chronik*, vol. 2, pp.187.

Plate A. Swiss Pikeman
Colour artwork by Giorgio Albertini © Helion & Company
See Colour Plate Commentaries for further information.

Plate B. Swiss Arquebusier/Handgunner
Colour artwork by Giorgio Albertini © Helion & Company
See Colour Plate Commentaries for further information.

Plate C. Swiss Hornblower, Canton of Zurich
Colour artwork by Giorgio Albertini © Helion & Company
See Colour Plate Commentaries for further information.

Plate D. Swabian League Master Gunner
Colour artwork by Giorgio Albertini © Helion & Company
See Colour Plate Commentaries for further information.

Plate E. Swabian League Landsknecht Pikeman
Colour artwork by Giorgio Albertini © Helion & Company
See Colour Plate Commentaries for further information.

Plate F. Swabian League Standard Bearer
Colour artwork by Giorgio Albertini © Helion & Company
See Colour Plate Commentaries for further information.

Plate G. (Clockwise) Banner of the Canton of Bern, Standard of a company of Swiss arquebusiers, Standard of Imperial cavalry of Maximilian I and Standard of the Swabian League
Colour artwork by Giorgio Albertini © Helion & Company
See Colour Plate Commentaries for further information.

**Plate H.
The Battle of Dornach
(Schlacht bei Dorneck)**

See Colour Plate Commentaries for further information.

Three Jews were among the captives.[26] One of them was a well-known good shot with an arquebus. Despite the weapon's reputation for inaccuracy, the Jew shot and killed the Master of Artillery from Fribourg, the standard bearer from Sursee, and others who were killed or wounded.[27] The Swiss decided that they had to do something with the Jew. Three suggestions were given regarding his fate. One man wanted him tortured and killed, another wanted him cast into perpetual prison, and a third wanted the captive spared to teach him how to shoot so well.[28] The hapless man was handed over to the men from Fribourg who seemed to want revenge and they tortured and killed him. They hanged him by his feet from a tree. After

The Campaign Against Liège. Woodcut based on a drawing by Hans Springinklee depicting close infantry combat. (Metropolitan Museum of Art, Harris Brisbane Dick Fund, 1928)

26 Dietrich von Endlisberg an Freiburg vor Tiengen 18 April 1499 in *Aktenstücke*, pp.142–143.
27 Anshelm, *Berner-Chronik*, vol. 2, p.187.
28 Lenz, *Schwabenkrieg*, p.102a.

he had hung a day and a night (or two days) the unfortunate man began to beg, saying that he had been converted to Christianity; he said that Saint Mary had appeared to him, and he wanted to die as a good Christian, he also confessed and acknowledged his sins. The executioner from Fribourg put the poor man out of his misery by beheading him while he was still hanging from the tree.[29]

An Exhausting War

As the war progressed, it became necessary for the Swiss to keep men in the field even though they often suffered from a lack of provisions. In 1499, the men of Wil changed the members of its garrison at Schwaderloh every 14 days, even though some of the troops requested staying longer. This rate of rotation was possibly to make sure the men could look to economic matters at home, and it may also have been a means of making sure that the troops would have enough food. When the provisions that the men brought with them, usually in their packs or haversacks, were consumed, the troops were frequently unable to find enough to eat.[30]

The Swiss signalling system to warn of enemy activities proved to be used too often, showing perhaps that the Confederates were jumpy and prone to overreacting. There appeared to be a marked tendency during the Swabian War to use signals too readily; time and again men were called to muster only to learn that there was no danger or that no one seemed to know why they had been called to assemble.[31]

The war extended beyond officially sanctioned military action. At one point, 3,000 men from Lucerne and Zürich united to raid across the Rhine into Germany. They had no authorisation to do so, and they were recalled before they could do much damage.[32] In July of 1499 the forces of Solothurn were operating near Basel, and at the time, there was a group of men who had followed this campaign without orders to do so. The leaders of Solothurn were able to convince these unauthorised troops to return without further incident.[33]

During the Swabian War, when the pressure on the manpower of the small Swiss town of Wil was excessive, young boys were seen practising in the village. These children spent most of the day in the alleys and streets with their little flags and sticks as if they wanted to fight the Swabians. The chronicler of Wil looked upon this activity with a certain amount of affection because he said it was 'very nice' (*wol schyn*) to see them doing

---

29 Anshelm, *Berner-Chronik*, vol. 2, p187; Lenz, *Schwabenkrieg*, p.102a.
30 Anonoymous (Placid Bütler, ed.), *Wiler Chronik des Schwabenkriegs*, (St Gallen: Fehr, 1914), p.185.
31 *Wiler Chronik*, p.220.
32 *Wiler Chronik*, p.223.
33 'Hauptleute an Solothurn,' 26 July 1499 in *Aktenstücke*, p.396.

so.[34] One contemporary of the Swabian War, Jakob Wimpheling, reported that the sons of the Swiss only concerned themselves with war. They could barely walk before they started wearing combat feathers and began beating their drums heavily day and night. They carried daggers above their left knee, learned to walk around proudly, dressed themselves splendidly, and with their appearance, divulged a wild disposition.[35] Clearly, young boys were practising military formations and manoeuvres. Even though the nature of Swiss training and practice remains obscure among adults, the Swiss military effectiveness clearly demonstrated that the men spent much time mastering their weapons and in drilling in military formations.[36]

The Battle of Frastanz 20 April 1499

The Imperial forces planned to put pressure on the Swiss and their allies by building defensive positions near their borders that could be used as bases of operations from which they would strike at their enemy. In February 1499 the Habsburg forces, reportedly mostly men from Swabia and the Tyrol, constructed extensive fortifications across a mountain pass in the Walgau Valley. The Imperial forces strengthened the natural terrain with barricades, which were located near the village of Frastanz and extended to the base of the Royaberg Mountain – these areas are just east of modern Liechtenstein – the barriers were considered formidable, 'It was a strong, well-ordered defensive position as no one had ever seen before.'[37] The defenders dug ramparts and bulwarks and cut down large trees to make a solid defensive line. Within these defences, the troops cut crenels, or firing holes, where they placed artillery pieces making for a very formidable defensive position. Using the fortified area at Frastanz as a base of operations, the Habsburg forces began to launch raiding expeditions across the Rhine into the areas controlled by the Swiss and their close allies in an attempt to seize resources, to destroy territories, and to wear down their enemy's ability and willingness to resist.

The number of Imperial forces at Frastanz was large and reportedly numbered 14,000 to 15,000 men. These troops staged a large raid in the area on 26 March 1499, reportedly consisting of a large portion of the available manpower, perhaps 8,000 men both mounted and on foot. The troops started their march at two in the morning to advance on the Swiss in the dark. The direct distance to their first target was about 10 kilometres, but the men had to follow the poor roads of the period, and the actual

---

34 *Wiler Chronik*, pp.220–221.
35 Jakob Wimpheling as cited in Edward A. Gessler, 'Die Waffenübungen der Jungend in der alten Eidgenossenschaft mit besoderer Berücksichtigung Zürichs,' *Zürich Taschenbuch* 23 (1923), p.199.
36 Elgger, *Kriegswesen*, pp.260–264.
37 Brennwald, *Schweizerchronik*, vol. 2, pp.388–389.

THE SWABIAN WAR OF 1499

The First Flemish Rebellion, Liège. Woodcut based on a drawing by Hans Springinklee showing a body of handgunners/arquebusiers supporting a division of pikemen. (Metropolitan Museum of Art, Harris Brisbane Dick Fund, 1928)

marching distance could have been twice as far. In any case, the march of the infantry was strenuous.

The Austrians crossed the Rhine and overwhelmed the Swiss garrison at Werdenberg (near modern Buchs in Switzerland). The Swiss were heavily outnumbered, and the outcome of the fight was never in doubt. The skirmish cost the Swiss 70 dead, while the Swabians lost 100 men. During the fighting a Swiss pikeman from Glarus, Hans Wal, was cut off from his comrades, and his situation was desperate. He knew he would die when 20 heavy cavalry came to engage him, but in a skilful use of the pike, he was able to knock three of them off their horses. In an impressive act of knightly virtue and generosity, Nik (Niklaus) von Brandis rode forward and demanded Wal's surrender, assuring the valiant man he would be protected from being harmed or killed, and Hams Wal surrendered. Brandis then placed his captive behind him on the back of his horse and took him to Feldkirch near Frastanz. The knight honoured Wal's courage and military skill by giving the Swiss his personal letter and seal and sent him home.[38]

The Swiss peasants often held the enemy nobles in disdain, and they saw the knights as a political and military threat to their freedoms and independence. Yet the Swiss knew about the standards of chivalry, courage, honesty, and fair play that the knights were supposed to embrace, and they often used the term of knightly (*ritterlich*) as a coveted compliment. But the conduct of many of the Imperial troops was brutal indeed.

The foray continued, and the Imperial raiding party swung north and became more vicious. On the way, the troops plundered and burnt several Swiss villages belonging to St Gallen including the large village of Gams roughly five kilometres from Buchs. Some innocent non-combatants in the path of destruction were much less fortunate. The leaders of the contingent

---

38   Brennwald, *Schweizerchronik*, vol. 2, p.390 and Anshelm, *Berner-Chronik*, 2, p.160.

FIGHTING A COSTLY WAR

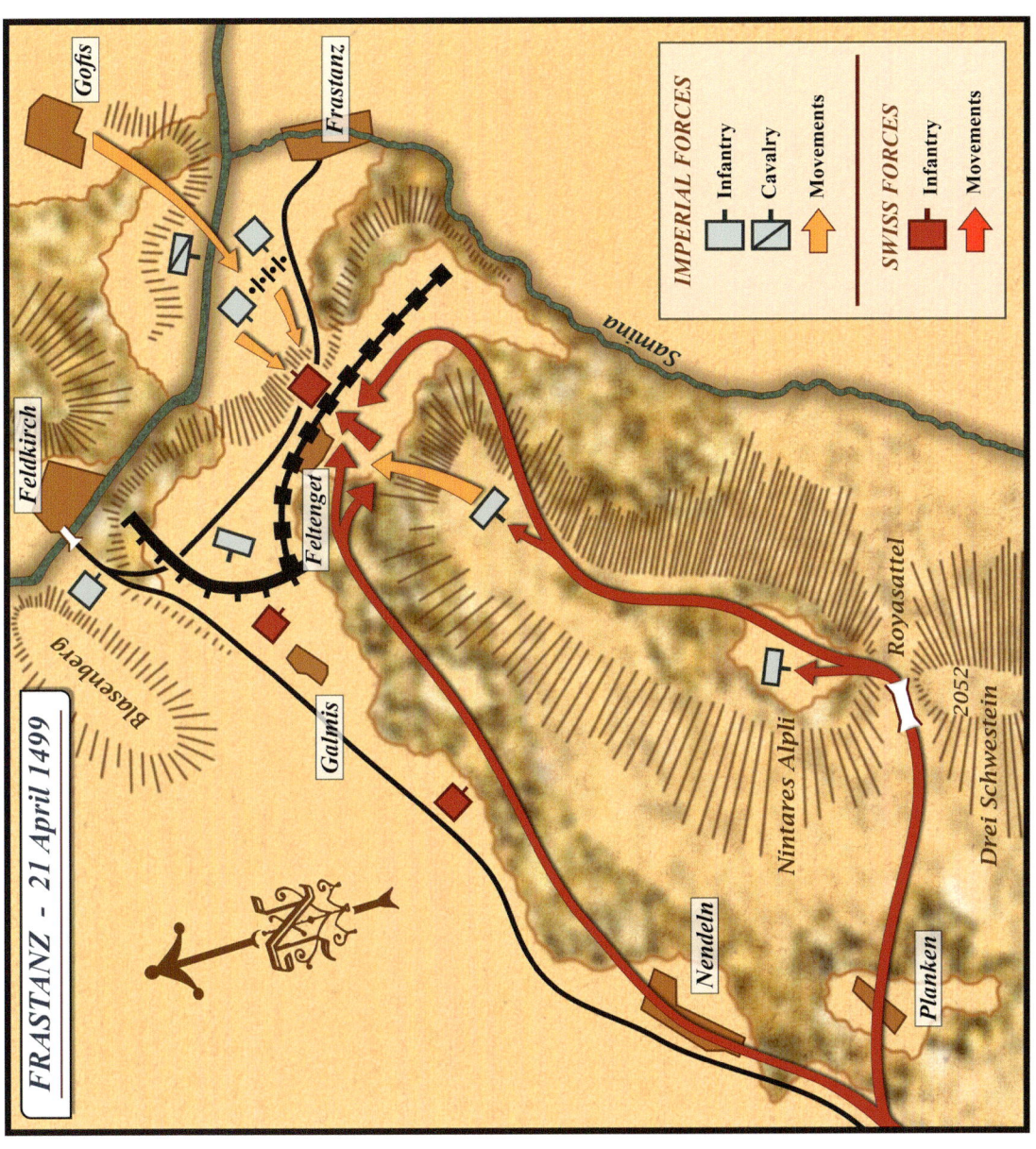

The Battle of Frastanz
20 April 1499

of troops from Zürich, Kaspar Göldi (*hauptmann*), and Rudolf Steinbrüchel (*venner*), wrote a letter on 29 March 1499, only three days after the Imperial raid, in which they succinctly described some of the most brutal atrocities of the entire war. 'The enemy came over the Rhine, have stabbed to death a number of women as well as many children and have cut off the male children's genitals (*gemecht*) and set fire to a number of churches.'[39] Modern researchers may suggest that Göldi and Steinbrüchel were mistaken or were exaggerating in their account.

Secure behind their walls of earth, wood, and stone, the Habsburg forces planned to launch more raiding expeditions across the Rhine into areas controlled by the Swiss and their close allies in an attempt to wear them down and perhaps goad them into attacking the defensive positions where the Imperial forces had a distinct advantage. The Swiss realised that the situation on the borders with the Tyrol was challenging as the successful raid and the brutal actions by the Imperial forces on 26 March had demonstrated. If the area was to be secure from future incursions, the Swiss would have to take definitive action against the fortifications at Frastanz.

The number of Imperial forces at Frastanz was large, and most of the reports state that 14,000 to 15,000 soldiers were stationed there. They were divided into three basic formations, two of infantry and one of cavalry. Most of the infantry was placed behind the fortifications, while the cavalry was held farther back to act as a reserve. The chronicler Valerius Anshelm states that the Habsburg forces numbered 14,000 men – a number repeated by another chronicler, Heinrich Brennwald.[40] These troops were largely hired to fight in the war, and many were Imperial troops from various areas of the Holy Roman Empire, including Tyroleans from nearby areas, the highly-regarded Swabian Landsknechts, as well as German mercenaries from elsewhere in The Empire. Troops also came from local areas including the Walgau Valley, no doubt reflecting animosities between the Swiss and their neighbours.

To stop further raids into their lands, the Swiss knew they had to neutralise the forces at Frastanz. The Confederates believed their chances of defeating the enemy were much better if they faced the Imperial Army in combat on open ground. In an attempt to lure the Austrians out of their defences, the Swiss besieged the important fortress of Gutenberg, opening the siege on 11 April. From the outset, the Confederates performed poorly. They had insufficient large cannon to reduce the walls of the castle, and one of the larger artillery pieces they did have blew up after firing only a few times. The attempt to undermine one of the towers was equally unsuccessful, and the Swiss efforts were so inept that they brought ridicule

---

39 Kaspar Göldli, Hauptmann und Rudolf Steinbrüchel, Venner, an Zürich, 29 March 1499 as cited in Brennwald, *Schweizerchronik*, vol. 2, p.388 in footnote.

40 Anshelm, *Berner-Chronik*, vol. 2, p.171 and Brennwald, *Schweizerchronik*, vol. 2, p.403.

from the defenders of the fortress. After eight days of the ineffectual siege, the Swiss realised they had failed to draw enemy forces from their defensive positions to engage the Confederates in battle.[41] The Swiss leaders decided that the only way to remove the threat of the Imperial forces was to storm their positions.[42]

The Swiss assembled their forces at Azmoos to take some decisive action. After the battle, the number of Swiss troops involved in the conflict was carefully listed, so the plunder taken after the engagement could be proportionately divided. The men from Zürich numbered 425, from Lucerne 600, Uri 720, Schwyz 1,410, Unterwalden 560, Zug 200, Glarus 622, Gaster 114 (or 113), Gams 48, Wagenthal 199, the city of St Gallen 553, the Lord of Sax 160, Appenzell 930, Grisons 1,600, Lands of the Abbey of St Gall 300, Werdenberg 196, Rapperswil 56, Toggenburg 651, Oberland [St Gallen] 487. The total was therefore 9,830 or 9,831 men.[43]

Wolleb, who was from Uri, was a man of considerable military skill and determination. He knew how to enforce discipline on his troops, and he expected a great deal from them. On 6 February 1499 he led the first Swiss raid of the war in retaliation for Swabian insults. He also executed an all night march on Ragatz (modern Bad Ragaz), and he stood a force of 30 Swiss in order all night in the bitter cold from which some of the men almost froze to death.[44]

Ulrich von Hohensax commanded the entire Swiss and Grey Leagues forces in the area, but Wolleb planned the battle, and this latter considered a simple frontal attack on the enemy positions to be too dangerous. He believed that attacks by two forces cooperating had the best chance of success if their movements were properly coordinated. One would be a flanking column, which would strike the enemy behind the fortifications, while the main force would advance and stage a frontal assault on the Imperial breastworks. To accomplish this, the force making the flank attack would have to climb the high, and steep sloped, Royaberg Mountain and then descend on the Tyrolean left flank. Wolleb was given the command of this flanking column with 2,000 men, while Hohensax led the larger group to march directly on the Habsburg position from lower ground.[45]

---

41 Brennwald, *Schweizerchronik*, vol. 2, pp.392–393.
42 Kurz, *Schweizerschlachten*, pp.152–153. See also, 'Die Schlacht bei Franstanz 1499,' *Rheticus: Vierteljahresschrift der Rheticus-Gesellschaft* Jahrgang 21 (1999) Heft 2, pp.[93]–198.
43 Josef Müller, 'Heini Wolleb: Hauptmann der Urner, Held zu Frastenz im Schwabenkriege gefallen den 20. April 1499 daselbst' *Historisches Neujahrsblatt* (1898), pp.58–59.
44 '[Angriff der Eidgenossen bei Triesen]' in 'Freiburger Chronik des Schwabenkrieges' in *Aktenstücke*, pp.566–567 and 'Hauptmann, Fähnrich und Räte von Uri, jetzt im Feld, an die Hauptleute der II Bünde in Churwalchen,' 15 February 1499 in *Der Anteil Graubündens*, pp.105–106.
45 Anshelm, *Berner-Chronik*, vol. 2, pp.169–70.

THE SWABIAN WAR OF 1499

Print based on a drawing by the veteran Urs Graf showing a Landsknecht (left) and a Swiss pikeman (right). By 1500, the principal difference between the dress of the two soldiers were the style of sword carried, together with the St George's Cross slashing on the clothing of the Swiss and the St Andrew's Cross style slashing on the Landsknecht's garb. (Editor's collection)

During the night of 19/20 April 1499, Wolleb assembled his column and began to scale the Royaberg Mountain some 1,600 metres above the troops' position. The Imperial forces knew that the Swiss might attempt such a flanking manoeuvre, so they reacted swiftly when they learned of the enemy advance and sent reinforcements to the top of the mountain. Some forces were already stationed on the summit of the Royaberg Mountain, but additional reinforcements raced to their aid in the dark, and they had time to place themselves into good order before their enemy approached. The Tyrolean force reportedly numbered between 2,000 and 3,000 men, with up to 2,000 of them armed with arquebuses to meet any possible Swiss attack with a hail of bullets.[46] These troops were under the command of Lienhart Nenn von Nenzig.

The Swiss in the column marched through the night and stayed so close together in the ascent that there was a danger of them falling on each other's weapons, specifically, the pikes had to be handled with great care. The troops marched through thick woods and over fields of stone. After a great effort, they approached the crest of the small mountain. They formed in good order and knelt in prayer before continuing their advance because they knew they were shortly going into battle where many of them might be wounded or killed, and many men no doubt found the supplication for divine aid comforting.

As the Swiss troops reached the crest of the mountain, the Imperial troops armed with arquebuses unleashed a 'horrible' fire upon them.[47] These firearms were only effective at close range, so the Confederates were near enough to both see what the enemy was doing and also hear the commands to fire. Since the Swiss spoke dialects very similar to their adversaries, they knew what was going to be unleashed upon them. When Wolleb saw that the Tyrolean men with their guns were about to discharge a volley, he gave a highly unusual order telling his men to fall onto their hands and knees to present smaller targets, while the fusillade boomed harmlessly overhead. Once again at Wolleb's command, the column got up to force their adversaries off the mountain. Within a short distance, the Swiss engaged the 2,000 (or 3,000) Imperial troops. After a fierce contest lasting about 15 minutes, the Tyroleans broke and fled in haste down the mountain to the defences at Frastanz, leaving many dead from the action.[48]

The practice of falling down to the ground suddenly in the face of enemy fire was highly unusual. Such a tactic required exact timing and strict discipline to be effective. When the men were on the ground, they could not wield their weapons, and a determined enemy, who struck at that moment, would have enjoyed a significant advantage. Yet such an attack would be very difficult to pull off in a timely manner before the

---

46 Hauptmann Schürpf etc. an Lucerne 20 April 1499 in *Aktenstücke*, p.148.
47 Anshelm, *Berner-Chronik*, vol. 2, pp.169–70.
48 Anshelm, *Berner-Chronik*, vol. 2, p.170. 'Hauptmann Schürpf et cetera an Lucerne,' 20 April 1499 in *Aktenstücke*, pp.147–9.

THE SWABIAN WAR OF 1499

men could stand up again to defend themselves. Possibly, the men firing the arquebuses could have also adjusted their aim lower to hit the smaller targets near the ground, but such fire discipline might have been difficult to achieve. Their weapons tended to be inaccurate and used black powder as a propellant, such powder left a great amount of smoke in the air, and that residue often obscured the field of battle. As has been demonstrated for centuries, even well-trained and experienced troops tend to overshoot their targets in the heat of battle, and the men using an arquebus had little chance of making effective adjustments to hit men on the ground. Wolleb's practice of ordering his men to fall to the earth before enemy fire was potentially

Print based on a drawing by Sebald Beham of a Landsknecht, dated 1520. The style of clothing shown suggests a depiction of Landsknechts from earlier in the century. (Metropolitan Museum of Art, Rogers Fund 1922)

dangerous, but it also proved to be highly effective at a critical juncture at the Battle of Frastanz.

Initially, the Tyroleans at the field fortifications in the valley had little idea of what was happening on the slopes above them. They could hear the din of battle, but the resolution of the fighting was unclear until they saw their forces running down the mountain fleeing from their adversaries. The Imperial forces were divided into two groups of infantry and one of cavalry, which acted as the reserve, and they shifted their strength to receive the pending attack on their flank. Meanwhile, Wolleb placed his men in proper order again before marching down the mountain. After offering another prayer, the troops began their descent.[49]

While Wolleb's force began marching on the Tyrolean flank, Ulrich von Hohensax led the main force to strike the enemy fortifications frontally. The attack directly on the breastworks took time, and a Swiss participant stated that, 'they [the enemy] have given us a great resistance for two hours.'[50] Meanwhile Wolleb continued to lead his men to attack the Imperial forces on their flank. Wolleb's column advanced towards the hastily-prepared left flank of the Tyroleans. Once again, the Imperial arquebusiers fired their weapons in unison. The opposing forces were so close to each other that the Swiss could see and hear the Tyroleans being told to fire. Wolleb then ordered his men to again to fall on the ground to avoid the enemy volley, as the salvo boomed harmlessly overhead. The smoke from the firing momentarily obscured the field of battle, and the Austrians had every reason to believe that their adversaries had suffered heavy casualties from the first fusillade and ceased to advance.

The Tyrolean arquebusiers reloaded their weapons and prepared to fire again. Wolleb called to his anxious men to remain on the ground, ordering them to wait until their enemy fired a second time before attacking, stating, 'Not yet, dear Confederates, let another shot be fired, and then attack the vulnerable [enemy] as rapidly [as possible].' The Imperial arquebusiers then unleashed another 'large clap of thunder and hail [of bullets]' from their guns. The arquebusiers in the column stood, and fired their weapons, and the remaining troops, armed with pikes and halberds, stood and advanced. Wolleb, conspicuous at the head of the advancing forces, was hit by an arquebus bullet when he reached the enemy positions – shot in the throat, he died instantly.[51]

According to the contemporary German humanist, Willibald Pirckheimer, Wolleb's death was especially heroic. Wolleb was a most courageous man (*audacissimus*), who did not hesitate to give up his life

---

49 'Freiburger Chronik des Schwabenkrieges' in *Aktenstücke*, pp.590–2.
50 'Hauptmann Schürpf et cetera an Lucerne,' 20 April 1499 in *Aktenstücke*, p.148.
51 Anshelm, *Berner-Chronik*, vol. 2, p.171; Brennwald, *Schweizerchronik*, vol. 2, p.404; and 'Freiburger Chronik des Schwabenkrieges' in *Aktenstücke*, p.591.

for his country. He took a halberd, and he crawled under the pikes of the enemy. He then presumably used the halberd to push up a number of pikes, which hindered the use of the weapons, so that they could not be used against the attacking Swiss. Wolleb kept the weapons from being used until he was stabbed through many times. He finally lost his strength, fell to the ground, and died. At this critical junction, his heroic sacrifice allowed the Swiss to press into the breach, which caused the Imperial battle order to falter and break ranks.[52]

A contemporary Swiss version of Wolleb's death presented some different details. At the outset of the battle, Wolleb and another man left the main formation of the Swiss to advance ahead of the rest. They then approached the first ranks of the Imperial forces, and grabbed their pikes in a bundle in their arms, so that the enemy was unable to lift up or use their weapons properly. Both Wolleb and his companion were stabbed to death in that effort. In addition, Wolleb was shot through the neck by a cannon, presumably a small calibre weapon such as an arquebus.[53]

These accounts of Wolleb's death are quite similar to the stories of the death of Arnold von Winkelried at the Battle of Sempach in 1386, when he supposedly fell on the pikes of the enemy forcing a gap in enemy lines allowing the Swiss to press through for victory, but was killed in the effort. The story of Winkelried's demise was recorded long after the battle causing pragmatic historians to question its authenticity, but his alleged sacrifice may still be similar to some of the desperate courage the Swiss displayed at that battle.[54] The story of Wolleb is much more authentic, and the sacrifice of the leader from Uri may have indeed caused a breach in the enemy lines, which allowed his men to rush through the opening giving them a big advantage as the fighting further developed.

Some of the Imperial forces put up an impressive resistance as the Swiss attack progressed. Numerous men from the Walgau Valley, where Frastanz was located, had come to fight their old enemies and to protect their homes and families. Some of these troops were well advanced in years, and these men fought well and won praise from their adversaries. As a contemporary historian stated, 'There were many old, honourable men with grey hair and beards who stood like poles and fought [well].' Their defence was so bold and tenacious that the Confederates stated in all the wars they had fought in the last 100 years they had never seen such a courageous enemy. Yet the courage of these men failed to change the outcome of the battle.[55] The fate of the men from Walgau – death, flight, or capture – was not recorded.

---

52 *Wilibald Pirckheimer's Schweizerkrieg,* Karl Rück (ed.) (München: Akademie, 1895), p.86.
53 'Acta des Tyroler-Kriegs,' *Rätia Geschichtsforschende Gesellschaft von Graubünden,* (1869), vol. 4, p.130. Jecklin, *Der Anteil Graubündens,* p.58.
54 Theodor von Liebenau, *Die Schlacht bei Sempach: Gedenkbuch zur fünften Säcularfeier* (Lucerne: Prell, 1886), p.91.
55 'Acta des Tyroler-Kriegs,' p.130.

The contest at the fortifications was costly for the Imperial forces, and reportedly over 1,000 of them were killed there as the Swiss pushed through the barricades.[56] The cost to the defenders was already high, but the battle was not yet over, and many more were yet to die.

At the critical juncture in the battle, when the Swiss forces were pressing through the fortifications, the Imperial forces were not fully engaged. While the infantry tried to stem the Swiss attack, the cavalry stood idly by without participating in the conflict. If these cavalry had been properly committed at this decisive moment, the fight would have had another dimension entirely with a possibly different outcome. The cavalry had watched the contest without taking action because they did not want to disobey orders and because they thought it risky to attack a hill the Swiss had just taken. Only one of them, a man named Ilsing, who was brave and well respected, thought it shameful that the cavalry would hold back and watch the infantry do all of the fighting. Showing great courage, he spurred his horse towards the enemy, and admonished his fellow cavalry to do the same. Yet he called to them in vain, and no one followed him except his squire, who saw that the man was in danger, so stayed with him. When Ilsing saw that he and his squire were alone, he made a hasty retreat, but a ball from a cannon knocked his horse down and pinned the rider under the animal. When his squire saw Ilsing's predicament, he dismounted, and despite grave danger, managed to pull the knight out from under the animal and to safety.[57]

The Swiss and their allies pressed their attack without Wolleb, and the Austrian infantry were finally broken, putting the entire Tyrolean army into flight. As Nicolaus Schradin stated rather poetically, the Imperial forces fled 'just as dogs run after hares.'[58] During the war, the largest number of casualties were suffered by a defeated army, when it broke and ran. Men who stood in the line of battle receive fewer losses when they kept good order. When the troops saw the fight going against them, they knew their best chance of survival was to get away fast. Once order was lost, the men had little ability to defend themselves and could be easily cut down by determined pursuers. The Confederates took advantage of this lack of order among the Imperial troops and began killing their enemies as they fled. Unfortunately for the Austrians, their line of retreat was severely hampered by the River Ill at their back, which flowed along their only avenue of flight. There were no bridges over this section of the Ill, and the fleeing troops were forced to try to swim the river or be slaughtered on its banks. Many swam across the river to safety, but many others, encumbered by armour and heavy clothing, drowned in the attempt. So many died in the river that

---

56 'Acta des Tyroler-Kriegs,' p.130.
57 Pirckheimer, *Schweizerkrieg*, German, pp.142–3 Latin, p.87.
58 Nicolaus Schradin, 'Der Schwabenkrieg vom J. 1499 besungen in teutschen Reimen durch Nicolaus Schradin, Schreiber zu Lucern 1500,' *Der Geschichtsfreund* (1847), vol. 4, p.36.

a mound of their bodies reportedly washed up on the banks of the River Ill at Feldkirch.[59]

The Swiss captured four flags along with 12 artillery pieces and 500 arquebuses. The victors took two prominent men from Feldkirch and held them for ransom to get some reimbursement for the costly raids from the fortifications near Frastanz into the Rhine Valley.[60] After the battle, the Swiss and the men from the Grey Leagues took a number of Imperial wounded and treated their injuries. The Walgau Valley was then undefended and at the mercy of the Swiss and their allies, who could have easily pillaged and burnt the entire area. But then priests, women, and children, in an attempt to appeal to the better nature of the victors, came to beg for mercy. The Confederates extracted 8,000 Gulden from the area, and did little additional damage.[61] The victors remained on the field of battle for five days, destroying the fortifications near Frastanz and burying the large numbers of the enemy dead. The Swiss and their allies were ill prepared for a lengthy campaign deeper into enemy territory, because they lacked the necessary supply train and equipage. They had already achieved the goal of the campaign of destroying the enemy base of operations, and thus they soon departed.

The Austrian army suffered very heavy casualties, while the Swiss losses were very modest. The propagandists were soon at work as could be expected, and both sides in the conflict reported numbers that made their side look good, or at least not as bad. German sources indicated that the casualties on both sides were somewhat similar. Hans Ungelter stated, on 24 April 1499, that 800 Swiss died in the battle, while 2,000 from the Imperial forces were lost.[62] Georg von Emershofen claimed on the following day, 25 April 1499, that 800 to 1,100 men of the Imperial forced died while the Swiss lost from 700 to 800 men.[63] These numbers are completely inconsistent with the Swiss sources.

The victorious Swiss controlled the field after the battle and could make more accurate assessments on the numbers lost on both sides, and they gave very different figures to those of their enemy. Captain Schürpf from Lucerne, a participant in the battle, reported on the same day as the encounter that the enemy had suffered 'upwards of 3,000 dead stabbed to

---

59 Anshelm, *Berner-Chronik*, vol. 2, pp.171–2 and Lenz, *Schwabenkrieg*, p.114.
60 Brennwald, *Schweizerchronik*, vol. 2, pp.406–7; 'Heinrich [Ammann] Hauptmann der Bündner an Cur' 20 April 1499 in *Aktenstücke*, p.149; 'Zürich an Hauptleute, et cetera der Eidgenossen im Feld,' 21 April 1499 in *Aktenstücke*, p.152; and Etterlin, *Kronica*, p.241.
61 Schradin,'Der Schwabenkrieg,' p.37.
62 Hans Ungelter an Esslingen 24 April 1499 in *Urkunden zur Geschichte des Schwäbischen Bundes*, vol. 1, p.323.
63 Georg von Emershofen an Nördlingen 25 April 1499 in *Urkunden zur Geschichte des Schwäbischen Bundes*, vol. 1, p.324.

FIGHTING A COSTLY WAR

Five German Soldiers, print by Daniel Hopfer after a drawing by Erhard Schön, c. 1520. (Metropolitan Museum of Art, The Elisha Whittelsey Collection, The Elisha Whittelsey Fund, 1951)

death and drowned' while not a single man from Lucerne had been killed.[64] Heinrich Ammann, also a participant, claimed that on the day of the battle 1,000 Germans were killed and many more drowned in the river, while '8 or 10 [Swiss] men died'. He added, 'about 60 Confederates were [also] wounded,' but he gave no indication of the severity of their injuries or how many of them might have died later from their wounds.[65] The leaders of Zürich reported the day after the battle also that not a single man from Zürich had been lost, and only 10 Swiss were killed in total, but these commanders thought that a few more Swiss bodies could still be found.[66]

Ludwig Feer wrote that 'not more than 12 men had been killed, among them were Heini Wolleb and Hans Küry' (Küry was the head bailiff from Schwyz).[67] Nicolaus Schradin suggested that a few more deaths were possible when he stated succinctly, 'No more than fifteen men died.'[68] The Swiss contemporary chronicles also presented similar numbers on enemy losses. Valerius Anshelm stated that more than 3,000 foes were killed on the field of battle and over 1,300 were drowned in the river. Heinrich Brennwald

---

64 'Hauptmann Schürpf et cetera an Lucerne,' 20 April 1499 in *Aktenstücke*, p.148.
65 'Heinrich [Ammann] Hauptmann der Bündner, an Cur,' 20 April 1499 in *Aktenstücke*, p.149.
66 'Zürich an Hauptleute et cetera der Eidgenossen im Feld,' 21 April 1499 in *Aktenstücke*, p.152.
67 Ludwig Feer, 'Ettliche Chronickwürdige sachen durch Ludwig Feeren der Zytt Stattschryber zu Lucerne beschrieben, Anno 1499,' *Der Geschichtsfreund* (1845), vol. 2, p.145.
68 Schradin, 'Der Schwabenkrieg,' p.37.

also reported 3,000 enemy were killed or drowned.[69] Some reports give higher numbers of enemy dead. Johannes Lenz wrote that 5,000 Swabians were killed on dry ground, and no one knew how many were drowned in the river. Therefore, the most reliable sources on the battle clearly stated that the Imperial forces lost at least 1,000 dead and most possibly 3,000 or more. In comparison, the sources agree that the Swiss lost between 8 and 12 men.

These numbers indicate that the Battle of Frastanz was one of the most one-sided victories not only in the Swabian War but also in the entire history of the Swiss Confederation. Frastanz also compares favourably with the Battle of Morgarten in 1315 when around 1,500 to 2,000 enemy were killed for a loss of about 14 Swiss. If Morgarten may be considered one of the most disproportionate victories in military history, then Frastanz must also be placed in that category.

More than any other person, the credit for the victory at Frastanz must go to Heini Wolleb. He planned and executed the battle to perfection. He faced a series of difficult problems which he was able to solve thanks to a good plan and personal leadership, which included a brilliant tactical innovation. Twice, he avoided potentially heavy casualties by ordering his men to fall to the ground, a manoeuvre which took great discipline to execute and to still retain the force's tactical formation. Wolleb was without doubt a leader of considerable ability, and the greatest tragedy for the Swiss at Frastanz was the death of the leader from Uri. The Confederate leaders, faced with similar problems at the Battle of Calven one month later, accepted Wolleb's strategic battle plan of marching over a mountain to attack their enemy's flank but not his tactical execution, and this oversight cost them dearly. If someone of Wolleb's leadership ability and tactical genius had been available to give acceptance to the practice of falling down before enemy fire, the greater casualties at Calven and at numerous engagements in the following century might have been less severe.

The Battle of Calven, 22 May 1499

The victory at the Battle of Frastanz proved to be inconclusive as far as raids from fortified passes in the Alps were concerned, since the Imperials still held other fortified mountain locations from which they could launch more raids, and the frequency of these incursions increased. The Imperials had built another base of operations of earth, wood, and stone that stretched across a narrow meadow at the mountain pass of Calven near the borders of the Grisons. The name Calven was derived from Chalavaina or Chavalaina in the Romansh Language meaning smelter. These Imperial forces raided over large distances, while the residents of the Grey Leagues in the area

---

69 Anshelm, *Berner-Chronik*, vol. 2, p.172; Brennwald, *Schweizerchronik*, vol. 2, p.405.

FIGHTING A COSTLY WAR

ineffectively fought against them. The men of Grisons soon called upon their Swiss allies to join them in taking definitive action, and Confederate forces swiftly assembled in the area.[70]

The Imperial defences at Calven were formidable, and one contemporary chronicler from Grisons described them with admiration. They were 'made handsome, defensible, strong [and] high with good bastions, bulwarks, and firing holes (crenels) side by side such that no man had ever seen before for a long time.' They were there to punish the Grey Leagues to enable a march through the Münster Valley to burn and strip the area of anything of value.[71]

The Grey Leagues and their Swiss allies prepared carefully for the coming attack on the fortifications at Calven by jointly practising force deployment and tactics. When word came that the Imperial forces were soon to receive reinforcements, Grisons and their allies decided they needed to attack the Imperial positions before the new troops could arrive. The Swiss forces who arrived to help in the effort were comprised of detachments from the central and eastern states, but the largest contingent in the army by far was the men from the Grey Leagues. The total force numbered about 6,300 men.[72]

The Imperial Army numbered over 13,000 men. Most of them stationed near the swift flowing River Rambach, and the force was divided into three main groups, two of infantry and one of cavalry, but the troops were further deployed for effectiveness and flexibility. At least, 2,000 men came from the Adige River Valley, and troops from other areas of the Tyrol were with them. They were all stationed directly behind the formidable defences at Calven to meet the possibility

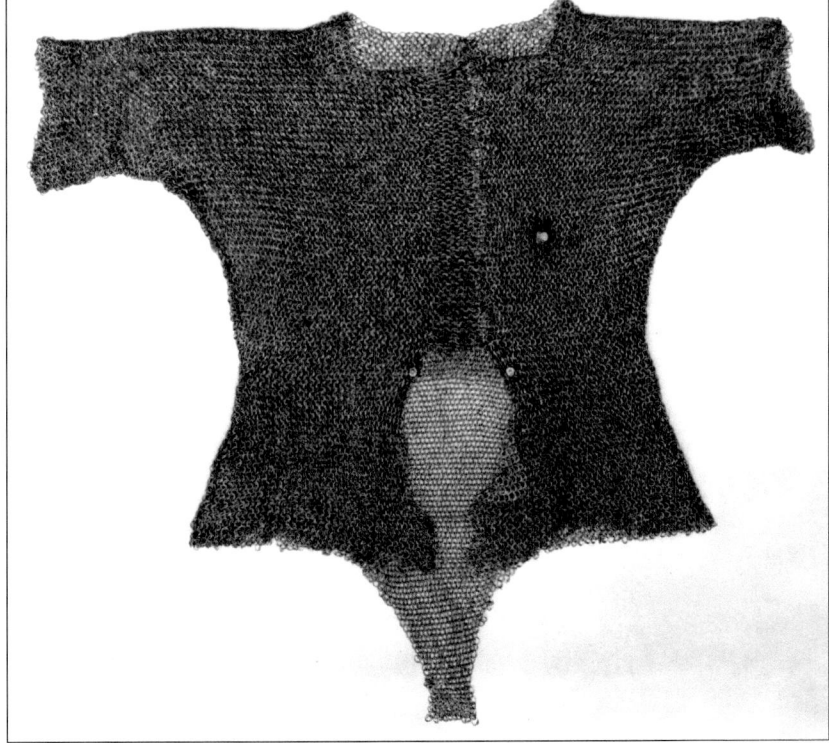

Mail hauberk, late fifteenth century, believed to have been made in Nuremburg (Metropolitan Museum of Art, Gift of George D. Pratt, 1925)

---

70 Jecklin, *Der Anteil Graubündens*, pp.61–63.
71 'Acta des Tyroler-Kriegs,' p.133.
72 Kurz, *Schweizerschlachten*, p.179; 'Acta des Tyroler-Kriegs,' p.133; 'Chronik von Johann Stumpf,' in *Der Anteil Graubündens*, p.34 and in the appendix.

THE SWABIAN WAR OF 1499

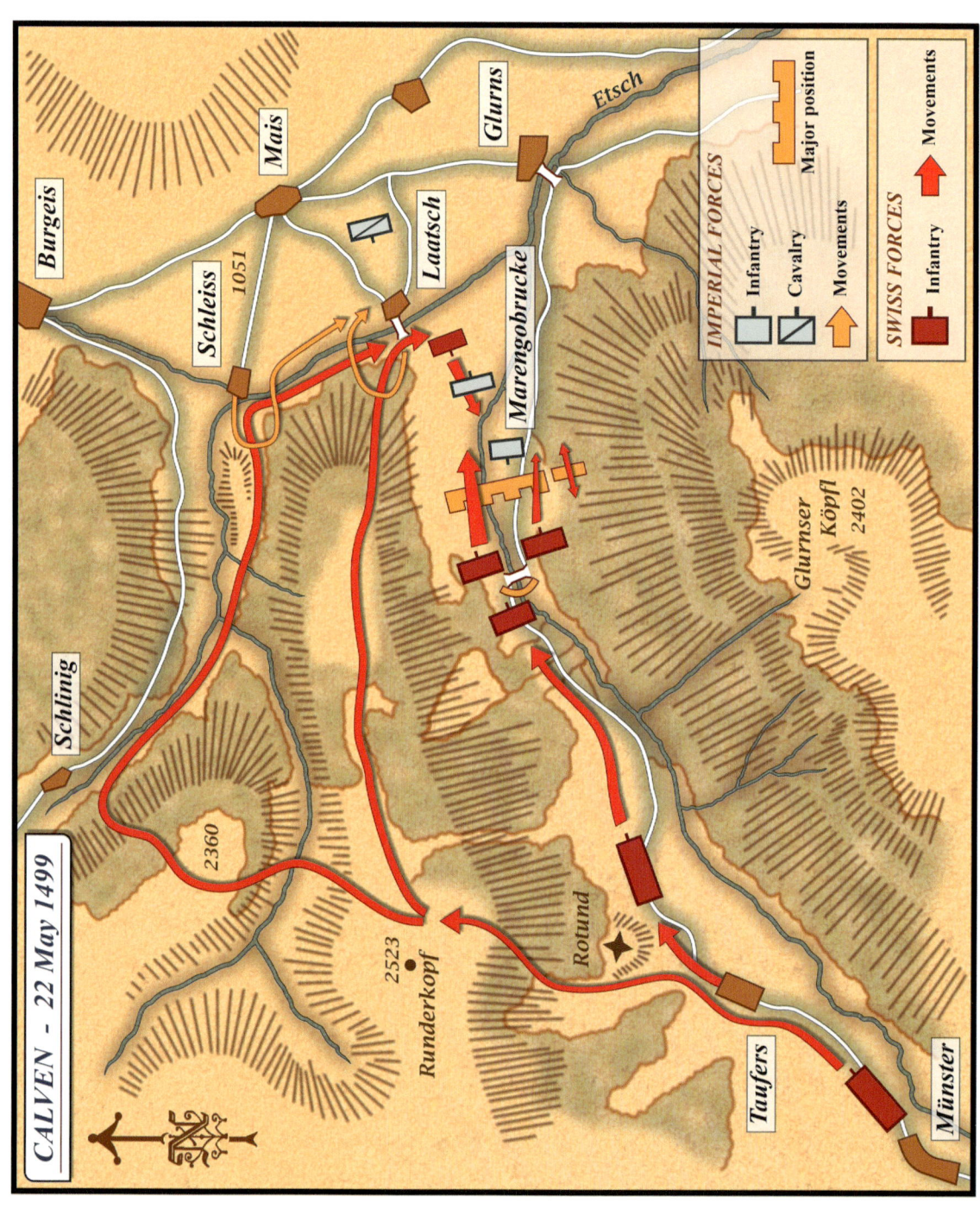

The Battle of Calven, 22 May 1499

of a frontal attack. Four contingents from Italy, numbering about 1,200 men, were placed to protect the left flank of the position. An additional 2,000 men, also from various areas of the Tyrol, were stationed between the fortifications and the river. The remainder of the army was placed farther back to function as a tactical reserve as needed, with the cavalry stationed on the flat area between the villages of Mals, Glurns, and Laatsch. The entire army numbered 13,000 men who were well supplied and armed, with numerous artillery pieces, and would prove to be very formidable opponents.[73]

The Swiss leaders planned a coordinated attack consisting of a flanking march and a heavy attack on the enemy fortifications similar to the battle plan at Frastanz. The flanking column was composed of between 2,000 and 3,000 men under the joint leadership of Wilhelm von Ringk and Niclaus von Lumbrins. Their route would take hours to complete, so they left in the night to be in position to attack the next morning. Such a nighttime advance was more likely to go unnoticed because the garrison at the enemy fortress at Rotund could observe their progress only in the daylight. Shortly after midnight on 22 May 1499 the flanking column began its 1,100 metre ascent of the mountain. The march was difficult in the darkness and covered roughly 10 miles through rugged and thickly forested terrain.[74]

After the flaking column had completed its march, men placed a white flag on a hill, and set a building on fire to signal the main force to attack the enemy fortifications. The flanking column met an Imperial column who attempted to keep it from crossing the Marengbrücke (Mareng Bridge). The Imperial forces held their ground in the face of repeated attacks by the Swiss and men of the Grey Leagues. Both Ringk and Lumbrins were killed while leading their men, but the fighting still continued without them, and casualties mounted. The action continued for hours with the Swiss unable to dislodge or defeat their adversaries, while suffering 200 dead and wounded. The Confederates and their allies were slowly being worn down, and their condition became dangerous. The fight lasted five hours and disaster was only avoided because the Imperial cavalry did not participate in the action. During the whole battle, the cavalry was the single force that could have saved the day for the Tyroleans, but it simply stood still at a distance for some unknown reason.[75]

The main force of the Swiss and their allies saw the smoke from the signal fires but hesitated to attack. Under the influence of the leader from Schwyz, Dietrich Freuler, they decide to delay their advance, so the flanking column could draw more Imperial troops from the fortifications, but they did not know about the precarious situation of the other forces until a runner arrived telling them it was in danger. Under the command of

---

73 Kurz, *Schweizerschlachten*, pp.179–180.
74 Lenz, *Schwabenkrieg*, p.121; Rieter, 'Schwabenkrieg,' pp.141–142.
75 Kurz, *Schweizerschlachten*, p.163; Brennwald, *Schweizerchronik*, vol. 2, p.420; Rieter, 'Schwabenkrieg,' p.142.

Benedikt Fontana and Hartwig Capauls, the main Swiss and allied force was divided into three pike bodies. These formations had to march for an hour and a half to reach the enemy defences.[76]

From the outset of their approach against the enemy defences, the Swiss and men from the Grey Leagues suffered a great deal from enemy fire. Arquebuses and cannon both took a heavy toll on the Confederates. The artillery pieces knocked great gaps in the advancing formations, and a single shot killed seven men including four brothers. The Confederates moved along the defences seeking a weak point where they might break through. Time after time, they attacked the fortifications only to be thrown back with heavy losses. In the heat of battle, the Imperials expended ammunition at a rapid rate, and they were forced to grab stones from the ground to continue to fire. Dietrich Freuler, the leader from Schwyz, commanded a group of volunteers or mercenaries who were hired by Grisons to support its war effort. As the leader of an elite group, he was expected to do well in battle, but he failed to do so. He delayed the advance of his column making a unified attack by the men of the Grey League more challenging. Rather than face the dangers of combat, Freuler abandoned his command and rode away 'from his men' and 'thus fled from them,' leaving the scene as a coward. Benedikt Fontana stayed with his command and led his men bravely until he was killed in the attack.[77]

The death of the popular Fontana helped turn the tide of the battle. Inspired by the thought of avenging their fallen leader, the Swiss staged a final heavy assault. Attacking over the bodies of their fallen comrades, and under heavy fire, the Confederates and their allies were finally able to force a gap in the enemy lines. The Imperials did not flee at first but bravely held their ground until the Confederates poured through in large numbers. Further resistance was then hopeless, and the Imperial forces began to break and run. Soon the whole army was in flight.[78]

The force, that had so long kept the Swiss flanking column at bay, also fled. The Swiss and their allies pursued the Imperials killing any of them they could overtake. The Confederates gave no quarter, and no prisoners were taken. Many men fled to the Marengbrücke, and a huge mass of men became jammed on the bridge which collapsed under their weight, causing many to fall into the river below. The Swiss and the men from the Grey Leagues pursued the Imperials for the rest of the day, hunting men down in the forests and killing them whenever possible. The slaughter of the fleeing men gave the Imperial forces their worst casualties of the battle. Reportedly,

---

76   Brennwald, *Schweizerchronik*, vol. 2, p.420 and Rieter, 'Schwabenkrieg,' p.143.
77   Jecklin, *Der Anteil Graubündens*, pp.71–2 and Lenz, *Schwabenkrieg*, p.117 and p.122.
78   Kurz, *Schweizerschlacten*, p.164.

4,000 Austrians and 2,000 Swiss and men from the Grey Leagues were killed that day, making Calven the most costly battle of the war.[79]

The Swiss and their allies were infuriated because of the heavy casualties, and they took revenge on the people in the area because they were German and loyal to The Empire. The Confederates took seven villages, including Glurns and Mals, and burnt them to the ground, not sparing a single house. The Swiss soldiers, with a number of priests, plundered the area taking or destroying everything of value, then they went on a killing rampage. They killed every male over 12 years of age, and they cut to pieces the bodies of 33 wealthy men from Meran. The Imperial losses in the battle, and presumably also in the following slaughter, was so extensive that 944 widows were much later reported in the Vingstgöw and among these were 150 in the Italian city of Meran (Merano).[80] The sound of crying and wailing filled the whole area near the battlefield as children wept for their fathers and women for their husbands. The Swiss and their allies buried their dead in two mass graves but left the enemy dead to rot where they had fallen. The Confederates did not long remain in the area, choosing to withdraw as the Imperial reinforcements approached.[81]

Clearly, Dietrich Freuler had disappeared during the battle, probably in flight. Also, his actions in hesitating to support the attack on the Imperial defences properly, brought great anger from many people who accused him of supporting the enemy. He was quickly arrested and thrown into jail in a public house in Chur. Yet he soon succeeded in escaping, and obtained sanctuary in the church of the city, from which, according to church law, he could not be forcefully removed. By the use of a clever trick he was able to deceive and then to elude the guards watching the church. He then sought sanctuary in Pfäfers outside the boundaries of the Grisons. Even though many still considered him a traitor, others said he had conducted himself properly during the Battle of Calven, and they went so far as to send a recommendation to Maximilian against whom he had so recently fought. Freuler was released and he continued his life as a mercenary. He is last recorded in 1513 as a soldier for the Swiss at the Battle of Novara, where he had robbed a rich Jew.[82]

The areas bordering the Grey Leagues and the Tyrol experienced considerable military activity in the weeks following the Battle of Calven, but no major engagements took place in the region. Maximilian personally led an expedition in the area in late May and early June. The Swiss did not meet him in battle, but they burnt everything before him as he approached,

---

79 Brennwald, *Schweizerchronik*, vol. 2, p.421; Lenz, *Schwabenkrieg*, p.123; and Rieter, 'Schwabenkrieg,' p.143.
80 'Acta des Tyroler-Kriegs,' p.138.
81 Brennwald, *Schweizerchronik*, vol. 2, p.422; 'Acta des Tyroler-Kriegs,' p.138; Lenz, *Schwabenkrieg*, p.123; and 'Willibald Pirckheimers Schweizerkrieg Deutsche Uebersetzung' in *Der Anteil Graubündens*, p.25.
82 Jecklin, *Der Anteil Graubündens*, p.82.

and skirmished with the Emperor's foraging parties. His army was soon starving and was forced to withdraw. Maximilian then turned the focus of the war farther west.[83]

Calven was based on a sound battle plan, but it faltered in the execution because the attacking columns, which were supposed to strike the enemy frontally and on the flank, failed to coordinate their efforts. The delay in the main column attacking the Imperials allowed them to meet the two threats one after the other, and heavy casualties were the price of this failure. The largest mystery surrounding the battle is the non-participation of the Imperial cavalry. At critical junctions in the action, heavy attacks by the cavalry could have altered the outcome of the battle, especially in view of the fact that the Swiss and their allies only won a narrow victory as it was. The famous distrust between the upper-class knights and cavalry and the peasant infantry may have been a factor, and the nobility might have just let the peasantry fend for themselves.

The flanking column of the Swiss and men from the Grey Leagues must be admired for their endurance. Carrying heavy weapons, the troops climbed 1,100 metres, marched 16 kilometres in six or seven hours and soon after fought a five hour battle. This column was composed of the most vigorous men available, but their physical performance was certainly admirable. From this and other examples, it was easy to understand why the Swiss troops were so prized and respected during the period.

The Destruction of the Engadin Valley, June 1499

Maximilian had recently been in the Low Countries looking after his interests there, but he then proceeded into the Tyrol to oversee operations more closely. He assembled his much-awaited and much-feared forces and marched to aid his men near Calven with an army numbering roughly 7,000 men including about 700 cavalry. On 22 May, the same day as the battle, his army reached Landeck nearly 72 kilometres from the battlefield – far too late and too far away to participate in the fight. Yet that distance could have been covered in a hard march by the cavalry in one day. If the cavalry had undertaken such a dash, and arrived in time, they could have helped the Imperial forces in the fight and perhaps influenced the outcome of the battle. When Maximilian heard of the result of the battle, he sent orders for the required workers to rebuild the destroyed fortifications including 1,400 men to dig with picks and shovels, 100 carpenters, and 100 masons. These men were assigned to build a redoubt at the former Imperial position that could be defended from every side if attacked. It is unknown if his plan was carried out. Clearly, the Emperor failed to realise that the old plans had become inadequate to the new conditions, and that the rest of

---

83   Rieter, 'Schwabenkrieg,' p.144.

FIGHTING A COSTLY WAR

the campaign would involve the movement of troops rather than defending static positions.[84]

After a fairly slow march of roughly nine kilometres a day, possibly slowed by the hauling of artillery pieces over rough roads, Maximilian and his army arrived in Glurns eight days after the Battle of Calven. When the Emperor saw the unburied bodies of men from his army, he praised them for their courage because so many of them had died of wounds in the chest and not in the back, but he wanted revenge against the peasants who had inflicted the defeat on his army.[85]

The 7,000 men Maximilian brought with him had been thrown together and were drawn from various garrisons in the areas of the Tyrol and contingents from the Imperial cities of Germany. This included a detachment of cavalry from Nuremberg led by the later humanist and historian, Willibald Pirckheimer. No doubt, numerous men came from remnants of the scattered Imperial forces, which had survived the Battle of Calven. But the Emperor still had 10,000 men in his command, and he wanted revenge for the recent defeat. He also hoped he could bring the peoples of the Grey League to terms and to do him fealty if he

A Swiss Soldier, attributed to Niklaus Manuel Deutsch, early sixteenth century drawing. (Metropolitan Museum of Art, Bequest of Walter C. Baker, 1971)

---

84   Jecklin, *Der Anteil Graubündens*, p.84.
85   Jecklin, *Der Anteil Graubündens*, pp.84–85.

THE SWABIAN WAR OF 1499

successfully campaigned down the long alpine valleys of the Engadin in Grisons.[86]

The Emperor had to be very concerned about supplies, and most importantly, food for his men. The mountain valleys had been so thoroughly plundered that there as scarcely enough nourishment for the people who lived there. Presumably, many had already fled the area as refugees, and had located elsewhere. The Imperial officials in Salzburg, Austria, were supposed to supply the needed sustenance, but they were overworked and out of funds, and they provided little support. Despite the weaknesses in his supply system, Maximilian pushed forward with his plans, and he directed the most unfortunate campaign of the entire war, the invasion of the upper Engadin Valley.[87]

Soon after Maximilian arrived in the area with his large army and established a camp, he made his headquarters at the Abbey of Marienberg where he held a council of war. He sought advice on how he could get revenge for the recent defeats of his forces, and his councillors expressed different opinions. The Emperor realised that storming the high mountain fortresses controlled by the men of the Grey Leagues would be most challenging. He also understood that cavalry would be relatively useless on the steep mountains slopes, so he would campaign without the heavy cavalry. Rather, he chose 15,000 infantry to advance against his adversaries. Maximilian knew he had limits as a military commander, so he turned operational control of the campaign over to Johann Truchsess von Waldburg, Count von Sonnenberg. Yet Maximilian was still heavily involved in planning the initial movements of the operation, and he sent for Willibald Pirckheimer, the captain of the cavalry contingent from Nuremberg. The Emperor then ordered Pirckheimer to deploy a party of 200 men to lead the advance of the Imperial Army. Pirckheimer participated in the campaign and presented an impressive and detailed eyewitness account of the devastation and cost of the war.

Very early in the campaign, Pirckheimer and his men came to an area of that had been severely ravaged. Clearly, the region had either suffered from the raids of the Imperial forces or from the retaliation of the men from the Grey Leagues. The area was possibly close to modern Müstair (Val Müstair). There, Pirckheimer witnessed and then described one of the most disturbing scenes of the entire war, when he came upon a village that had been burnt and completely destroyed.

> We met two old women driving about forty little boys and girls like a flock of sheep. All were starved to the most extreme emaciation and,

---

86 Heinrich Ulmann, *Kaiser Maxiliain I: Auf urkunlicher Grundlage Dargestellt* (Stuttgart: Gotta, 1884), vol. 1, p.760; Jecklin, *Der Anteil Graubündens*, pp.84–85.
87 Jecklin, *Der Anteil Graubündens*, p.86.

except that they moved, not unlike corpses, so that it was horrible to see. I asked the old women where they were leading their miserable herd. Hardly had they replied, when we came to a meadow. They turned in and falling on their knees began to eat grass like cattle, except that they picked it first with their hands instead of biting it from the roots. They had already learned the varieties of the herbage, and knew what was bitter or insipid, what sweeter or more pleasant to the taste. I was horrified at so dreadful a sight, and stood for a long time like one who cannot trust his senses.

Then the woman asked, "Do you see why this wretched crowd is led here? Well would it have been if none of them had been born .... their fathers have fallen by the sword, their mothers have died of starvation, their property has been carried off as booty, their houses burnt; we two wretches, tottering with age, are left to lead this miserable herd like beasts to pasture, and so far as we can, keep them alive on grass. We hope that a short time will relieve them and us from our miseries. They were twice as many, but in a brief time they were reduced to this number, since daily some die of want and hunger, far happier in a quick death than in longer life." When I had seen and heard these things I could not restrain my tears, pitying pitiable human lot, and detesting, as every true man ought, the fury of war.[88]

My less poetic translation of the last sentence from the Latin might be 'When I saw and heard [this], I could not hold back the tears in which the wretchedness of the human lot and the fury of war deserves to be cursed.'[89] Pirckheimer gave no further information on what happened to these children. Hopefully, the troops, their auxiliaries, or someone in the area gave them food and care.

The weather patterns in Europe in the late Middle Ages were colder than they are today, and snow was still found in the high mountain passes and the valleys of the area even in June 1499. The Imperial troops took a direct route in the high valleys, but they could hardly make progress on the march because of the slippery and steep inclines where they frequently had to march through soft snow and mud that stuck to their shoes. The *Engadiner* (the inhabitants of the Engadin Valley) waited for the army to approach the Casana Pass at 2,692 metres above sea level. There the men found the pass

---

88 Willibald Pirckheimer as cited and translated by Paul van Dyke, *Renascence Portraits* (New York: Charles Scribner's Sons, 1905), pp.318–319. Paul van Dyke quotes Pirckheimer, *Schweizerkrieg*, Latin, pp.98–99. See also Pirckheimer as cited in Wilhlem Oechsli, *Quellenbuch zur Schweizergeschichte* (Zürich: Schultheß, 1918), pp.242–243.
89 Pirckheimer, *Schweizerkrieg* Latin, p.99

covered with 'eternal snow', which obviously failed to completely melt even in the summer time.

The *Engadiner* stood in a line on the high slopes waiting for the advance of their enemies. To the Imperial troops, who were approaching at a distance, they looked just like 'a flock of very small birds.' Nevertheless, some of the men from the Grey Leagues left their formation, came forward, and rolled huge stones downhill to hinder the advance of the Imperial troops as much as possible. They had also dug under huge boulders and had taken logs to use as levers to release the stones to fall down the slope of the mountains, making a great sound as they did so. Yet these large rocks did little damage because many of them sank into the deep snow before reaching the troops. If the dislodgement and the rolling down of the stones had been more successful, it would have been nearly impossible for the Imperial forces to dislodge the men on the high ground. As it was, their enemies posed little danger. However, skirmishers on both sides engaged each other by throwing smaller stones and firing crossbows and arquebuses at each other. The men of the main body of the Imperial forces kept their formation and slowly advanced up the incline to the summit. At that point, the men of the Grey Leagues engaged the Imperial troops on the front and left flank, but they soon realised they were heavily outnumbered and withdrew after suffering heavy casualties. The Imperial troops kept their formation and then began to descend down the mountain.[90]

When the Imperial forces were making their descent, there was a very large snow bank, which had started to melt and had become soft in the sun's heat, and a large section of it broke loose and collapsed down the slope of the mountain. It fell about the distance of the shot of an arrow from a bow and swept away 400 soldiers who were engulfed into a deep mass of snow. It appeared at first to be a gruesome sight because so many men could have been killed and engulfed in this deluge of snow, but this concern soon turned to relief and laughter when the soldiers reappeared from the snow. But they had all lost their weapons as well as their helmets and shoes. As far as anyone could tell, no one was missing, although many men had been severely injured.[91]

Finally at dusk, the Imperial Army arrived in the Engadin Valley, which had many lovely decorated hamlets and villages, but the enemy had set fire to the bridge over the River Inn, which had to be used to cross the River. After the fire had, with great effort, been put out the men crossed and established a camp near the village of Schanf. When the men of the Grey Leagues saw that the enemy had crossed the bridge, they set the nearby village of Zuoz on fire to keep the Imperial forces from making use of it. That same night, the soldiers stayed in the village, exhausted and suffering

---

90 Pirckheimer, *Schweizerkrieg* Latin, pp.99–100; Pirckheimer in Oechsli, *Quellenbuch*, pp.244–245.
91 Pirckheimer, *Schweizerkrieg* Latin, p.100; Pirckheimer in Oechsli, *Quellenbuch*, p.245.

from hunger, because the troops of the Grey Leagues had either destroyed or carried off all foodstuffs in the area.[92]

At dawn the next morning, the Imperial forces advanced in the traditional three pike bodies (*haufen*). The lead formation, called the 'lost,' had four artillery pieces with it, which had been brought with great effort by men using ropes to drag them over the mountains. Then followed the main force which always kept its order well. The rearguard came next, which was assigned to protect the needed baggage, although some of it was also considered to be useless and bulky equipment that slowed progress. The *Engadiner* marched in front of the Imperial pike squares destroying and laying waste to everything. When the area was relatively level and appeared to be favourable for deploying troops, the men of the Grey Leagues would turn and form up as though they wanted to give battle. These troops could see that they were heavily outnumbered, and they knew they were too weak to meet their enemies in a full-scale engagement, so they would quickly retreat. It seems that these mock deployments were little more than an attempt to harass, tire, and distract the advancing forces.[93]

Meanwhile, numerous fires lit up the entire area, and everywhere the burning buildings collapsed with the sound of a great crash. The *Engadiner* had already burnt the villages of Schanf and Zuoz, and they soon also set fire to Madulain, Samedan, Celerina, Potresina, St Moritz, and the other small communities in the area all the way to the settlement of Sils im

Pavise, probably fifteenth century. Although this example is of Saxon origin, it is similar to pavises that would have been used by the Imperial forces during the Swabian War. The image on the face depicts St George. (Metropolitan Museum of Art, Bashford Dean Memorial Collection, Bequest of Bashford Dean, 1928)

---

92 Pirckheimer, *Schweizerkrieg* Latin, p.101; Pirckheimer in Oechsli, *Quellenbuch,* p.246.

93 Pirckheimer, *Schweizerkrieg* Latin, p.101; Pirckheimer in Oechsli, *Quellenbuch,* p.246.

Engadin, so the enemy could not use them. The Imperial troops finally made camp near a burnt-out village, and their leaders discussed what they should do the following day. They finally decided that they could advance no further because of a lack of supplies and the hunger of their men. The best course of action was to fall back the way they had come. The soldiers would simply have to endure the hardships of hunger.[94]

Early the next morning, the rank and file of the suffering army began the march as quickly as possible. This time the soldiers of the Grey Leagues did not fall upon the rear of the retreating soldiers, but hurried ahead of them and occupied the high ground to inhibit the march of the enemy troops or to overwhelm them whenever possible. If the army had advanced towards the positions held by the *Engadiner*, they could have fought at a disadvantage. After a long march, the Imperial troops finally reached the hamlet of Zernez at nightfall; Zernez had already been burnt early in the campaign. If the army had hesitated in the day's march the soldiers would have been placed in great danger, because when the residents learned of their approach, they began to dismantle the bridge that the army needed for its retreat. If this means of retreat had been lost then the troops would have died more from hunger than from battle. The men were only granted a short rest, and then they resumed their march early in the morning.[95]

Suffering from hunger and the sweat of their great exertion, the army finally crossed the saddle of the mountain by the end of the day, probably on 10 June 1499, and entered friendly territory, but they had suffered many losses. Some of the troops died from hunger, and others from the great hardships of the campaign. Their hunger had been so severe that men on the march pulled out grass from the ground and devoured it just like cattle. A few of the soldiers lost their reason because of hunger, went into a frenzy, and went completely insane. The troops had been helped through their ordeal by the fresh water that came down the mountains, but there was little food waiting for them when they got back to friendly areas. Even though, Maximilian had ordered provisions to be brought to the retreating men, the much-needed foodstuffs were not available because of the carelessness and neglect of the Imperial officials.[96]

A major problem for the Imperial forces for the entire campaign in the Engadin Valley was a lack of logistical support. Without the required supplies, the troops had to depend on what they could acquire from the villages and hamlets in the Engadin Valley, but the people from the Grey Leagues had removed or destroyed the needed foodstuffs. Additionally, Maximilian's army needed to be paid, and when little in the way of compensation was

---

94 Pirckheimer, *Schweizerkrieg* Latin, p.101; Pirckheimer in Oechsli, *Quellenbuch,* p.246.
95 Pirckheimer, *Schweizerkrieg* Latin, p.102; Pirckheimer in Oechsli, *Quellenbuch,* p.247.
96 Pirckheimer, *Schweizerkrieg* Latin, p.102 and Pirckheimer in Oechsli, *Quellenbuch,* p.247.

forthcoming, the men could only be rewarded by plundering the area and taking what booty was available, but once again, everything of value had been removed, burnt, or otherwise destroyed. Faced with these difficulties that proved to be insurmountable, Maximilian witnessed the complete dissolution of the army he had sent against the Grisons. Presumably the troops had no recourse but to leave the area either in search of employment as mercenaries elsewhere or to return to their homes. The Emperor soon left this theatre of the war and went over the Arlberg Pass to the Lake Constance area to direct the conflict from that location.[97]

The Swiss Federal Diet was slow to react to the threat posed by the enemy campaign in the Engadin Valley. After repeated requests from the Grey League, the Swiss finally decided to act. Due largely to the slow communications at the time, the Diet only decided to send reinforcements on 12 June 1499, when it stated that 4,000 men should be sent to help. Zürich was supposed to send 1,000 men. Lucerne would send an additional 600, and the remaining number would be supplied by smaller contingents from nine other Swiss cantons. All these men were required to take the field no later than 15 June 1499.[98] From 19 June to 22 June, the contingents from the various Swiss cantons assembled in Chur, where they were joined by 2,000 men from the Grey Leagues. Since the people of Grisons feared another incursion into their lands, this combined army of approximately 6,000 men then marched into the Engadin Valley.

By the time the Swiss and their allies entered the Engadin and the nearby valleys days later, the enemy was gone, and the campaign was much like a 'strike in the air.' They advanced through the areas that had so recently been the scene of much destruction, and they then learned that the Imperial forces were long gone. Marching almost entirely unopposed, they entered the enemy regions that had not been devastated by earlier campaigning. They passed the site of the Battle of Calven and reached a position roughly 20 kilometres from Meran (Merano). At this point, the men had second thoughts about continuing their advance. The mountain valleys were narrow, they did not know the terrain, and their governments failed to give them permission to go so far, so they turned around. By the beginning of July, the men had returned to their homeland, and they had left only a small garrison of 200 men on the borders of Grisons to give warning of any future advances of the enemy, but the military operations in the area were over.[99] The next major Imperial attempt to invade the Swiss Confederation soon took place farther to the west which resulted in the most decisive action of the entire war, the Battle of Dornach.

---

97 Frey, *Kriegstaten*, p.366.
98 *Amtliche Sammlung der ältern Eidgenössischen Abschiede*, vol. 3, p.615.
99 Frey, *Kriegstaten*, p.366.

A Defiant Swiss Girl

The Swiss war effort was supported by almost every aspect of society including women and girls, who often showed remarkable strength and cunning as was demonstrated by a meeting witnessed by Willibald Pirckheimer in Constance, who had come to the city after the Imperial campaign in the Engadin Valley.

Young women were often allowed to pass freely between the armies because they certainly posed no military threat. These 'immature girls' (*puellae immaturae*) kept a channel of communications open between the antagonists and carried letters negotiating the terms of release for prisoners. In July of 1499, a letter for Maximilian was brought to Constance by one of these Swiss girls. Willibald Pirckheimer witnessed the scene when the Emperor's men tried to intimidate the child into giving information on the Swiss army facing the city as she awaited a reply.

Someone asked the girl what the Swiss were doing. She answered:

Don't you see they are awaiting your attack?

She was then asked how many men the Swiss had. To which she replied:

Just enough to repel your advance.

And she added that the men in Constance could have counted the Swiss in a recent battle before the city gates if flight had not blinded their eyes.

She was asked whether the Swiss had enough to eat, to which she simply responded:

How are they able to live if they do not eat or drink?

One of the men clearly became angry at her defiant and insulting replies, and he tried to frighten the girl by threatening to decapitate her. When the girl saw this, she said,

Truly you are a hero that you threaten a young girl with death. If you have such a great desire to draw a sword, why don't you throw yourself on the enemy positions? There you will meet a man who will answer your courage. But it is easier to confront an unarmed and innocent girl than put yourself before an armed enemy who knows how to conduct himself not with words but with deeds.

Pirckheimer said he was delighted with the girl's answers as well as her courage and frankness.[100]

The Battle of Dornach, 22 July 1499

By July 1499, the war was going badly for The Empire. The Swiss had been successful in defeating the Imperial forces in every important engagement of the war, and The Empire's operations in the mountains of Tyrol and the

---

[100] Pirckheimer, *Schweizerkrieg*, Latin, p.112 and Pirckheimer in Oechsli, *Quellenbuch*, p.248.

FIGHTING A COSTLY WAR

Grey Leagues had floundered. Yet Maximilian could still be optimistic about the war's outcome. He had assembled large armies around Constance and in the Sundgau Valley near Basel. Most of the troops in those areas had not seen any major action, and many were still anxious to punish the Swiss and seek revenge for the Confederate raids. Yet any significant operations would have to take place soon because funds were nearly exhausted, the troops were complaining of a lack of pay, and some were already deserting to return home. A single key victory could secure enough booty to keep the armies intact, and such a success would doubtlessly strengthen Maximilian's war effort and might even convince the Swiss to come to favourable terms with The Empire.[101]

Maximilian's plan was to make a demonstration in one area to divert attention and then to simultaneously stage a significant strike in another. The largest Swiss force concentrations were around Constance, watching The Empire's troop movements very closely. A large advance in that area would attract a good deal of attention, but a demonstration of force from

Castle of Dornach, anonymous after 1810. (Rijksmuseum RP-P-2018-1751)

---

101 Eugen Tatarinoff, *Die Beteiligung Solothurn am Schwabenkriege bis zur Schlacht bei Dornach 22. July 1499* (Solothurn: A. Luety, 1899). See also, 'Gedenkschrift 500 Jahre Schlacht bei Dornach 1499–1999,' *Jahrbuch für Solothurnische Geschichte* (1999), vol. 72, pp.5-[392].

Constance should not risk battle because a defeat might break up or even destroy the Imperial Army. The main attack would take place farther west, and Maximilian ordered Heinrich von Fürstenberg to advance from the Sundgau to take the Castle of Dorneck in the Birs Valley near Basel. Dorneck was a strategic focal point for a large area of the Swiss Confederation. From there, an army could march west to the Jura mountain passes, southwest to Bern, south to Solothurn, or east to Olten, and from Olten, down the Aara Valley to the Zürich area.[102]

In May and June 1499, Fürstenberg assembled his army in the Sundgau Valley of southern Alsace. It numbered between 10,000 and 15,000 men, but these troops varied greatly in quality. Many were simple conscripts who had little interest in the campaign or its outcome. Others were the superb Landsknechts from Gelderland, able and experienced German mercenaries numbering over 2,000 men. The infantry was armed in a similar fashion to the Swiss with long pikes and other shorter weapons such as halberds. The army had a number of large artillery pieces for sieges and smaller guns to be used in battle. The cavalry consisted of 1,100 of the feared and respected '*Welsch*' Guard from Burgundy. However, due to lack of pay, these cavalry were poorly motivated and proved to be largely ineffective in battle because they were more interested in taking booty than in the conflict.[103]

Fürstenberg could have marched on Dorneck early in July and met little resistance, but he decided to await the arrival of more horse, thus allowing the Swiss more time to react to his threat and prepare a better defence. Solothurn had purchased the Castle of Dorneck in 1490, and the city recognised the strategic value of the fortress and garrisoned it throughout the war. Benedikt Hugi led the small garrison of slightly more than 20 men, and their commander was concerned about his ability to protect the castle in case of attack. He wrote to Solothurn frequently requesting more men and support. The city finally reacted on 9 July 1499 and sent masons to repair the castle and artillery pieces to strengthen its defence, but these preparations were unfinished when the enemy army arrived.[104]

Solothurn sent its mayor, Niklaus Conrad, and 1,500 men to Gempen, a village about four miles from Dorneck, to watch the area and harass the Imperial forces should they advance. A Swiss army of 6,000 men was watching the enemy forces at Constance, but the demonstration from that fortress was unimpressive, so Solothurn was able to convince them that the greatest danger was at Dorneck. When the Confederates at Constance heard that Fürstenberg's army was approaching the castle near Basel, most

---

102 Lenz, *Schwabenkrieg*, p.136.
103 'Anonyme Chronik des Schwabenkrieges' in *Basler Chroniken*, 7 vols. (Leipzig: Hirzel, 1872–1915), vol. 6, p.11; Anshelm, *Berner-Chronik*, vol. 2, p.218; Tatarinoff, *Beteiligung*, pp.166–7; Reiter, 'Schwabenkrieg,' p.146.
104 Anton Haffner, *Chronica* (Solothurn: Zepfel, 1849), pp.58–59; Elgger, *Kriegswesen*, p.388; Anshelm, *Berner-Chronik*, vol. 2, p.192; Rieter, 'Schwabenkrieg,' p.145.

FIGHTING A COSTLY WAR

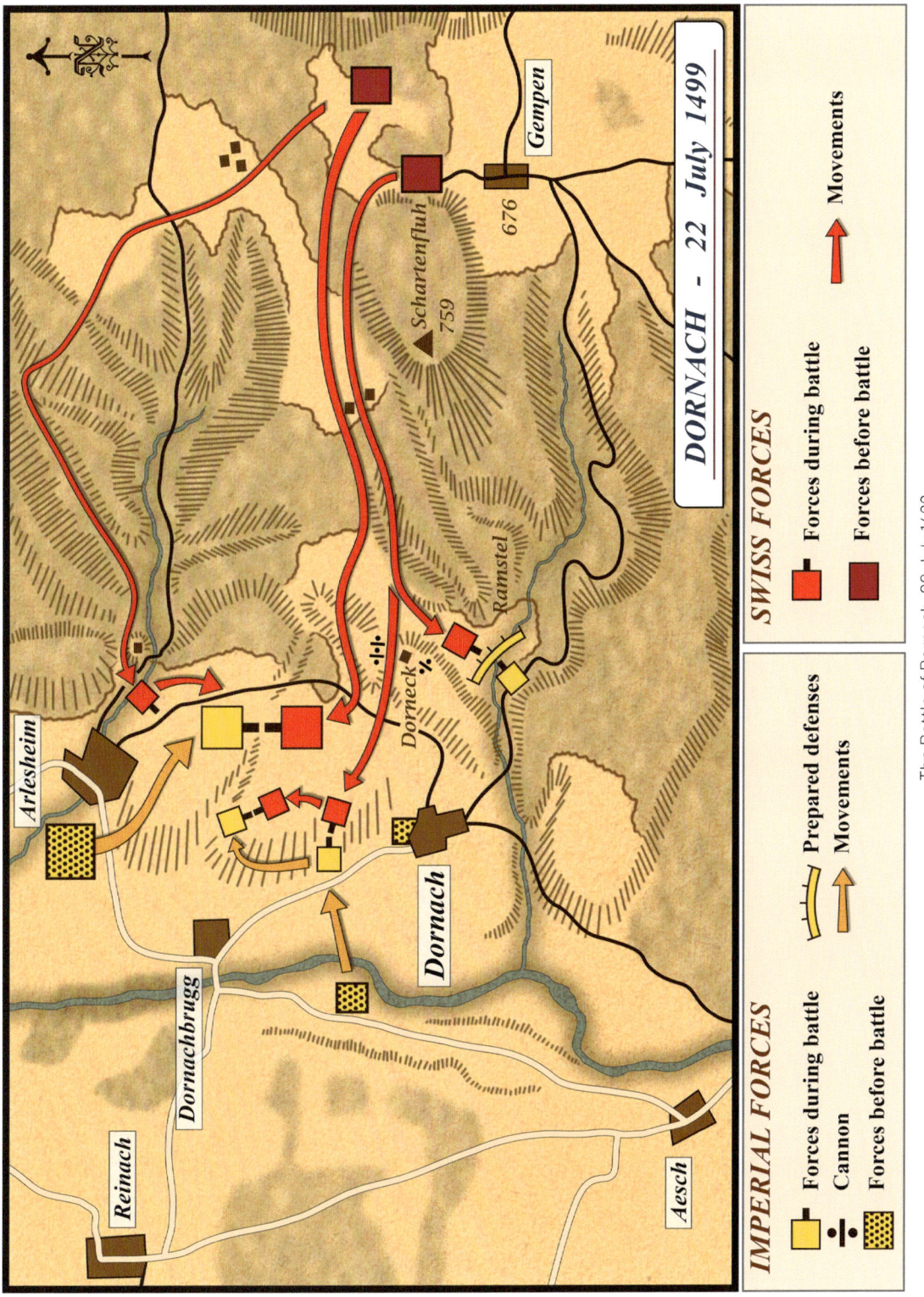

The Battle of Dornach, 22 July 1499

of them marched to Gempen as rapidly as possible. For the first time in the war Bern, angered by Swabian raids, sent a large contingent of 3,000 men to help Solothurn. On 20 July 1499, the Swiss contingents began to reach Gempen.[105]

The Imperial Army started to arrive near Dorneck early on 22 July 1499, and those troops began to prepare a siege according to all the accepted practices of the age. The nearby villages, including Dornach, had already been destroyed during a raid in March, so these forces could not plunder the area. The date was St Mary Magdalene's day, and the army took advantage of the holiday. The men played games, danced, and sang in the fields between the villages of Dornach and Arlesheim. Only the artillerymen were busy because they had to dig into the ground to lay the largest siege cannon on the correct trajectory to hit the castle while absorbing the recoil of the weapons at the same time. Smaller artillery pieces were placed around the castle to shoot in various directions in case of an enemy advance. Guns were also placed on the road between Dornach and Gempen to ward off any possible Swiss attack by that route, but this was the only real precaution taken against the possibility of a surprise attack. Fürstenberg's men failed to place guards and to send scouts to reconnoitre the area. A man from Basel came to warn the troops that Swiss forces were nearby, but his timely caution was ignored.[106]

Niklaus Conrad could see the entire Imperial Army from the Schartenfluh Hill, and he believed that a surprise attack in sufficient strength could be successful, although all available manpower would need to be present to make such an effort. Additional Swiss troops started to arrive in the morning, but they were tired, hungry, and wet with sweat from their long marches. By the early afternoon, they numbered over 5,000 first-class troops. Among them were 3,000 Bernese troops and another 400 from Zürich. The men from Solothurn shared food and wine with these men, and they were given some time to rest.[107]

The only groups that were still on the march were 600 men from Lucerne and 400 from Zug. The Swiss council of war decided to go into battle without these additional men because if the attack were long delayed there would be little chance of concluding the battle before nightfall, but they hoped that the expected contingents would arrive in time to aid in the outcome of the battle. The Confederates advanced in two pike squares, a *vorhut* (vanguard) and a *gewalthaufen* (main body) believing that the men from Lucerne and Zug would comprise the *nachhut* (rearguard) when they arrived. To avoid detection, the men marched through the forest instead of using the road. The Swiss began their advance in the mid-afternoon.[108]

---

105 Anshelm, *Berner-Chronik*, vol. 2, p.218 and pp.224–225.
106 Etterlin, *Kronica*, p.250.
107 Kurz, *Schweizerschlachten*, p.169; Lenz, *Schwabenkrieg*, p.152.
108 Tatarinoff, *Beteiligung*, p.175.

Niklaus Conrad was the commander of the vanguard, comprised mostly of men from Solothurn. When this formation advanced out of the forest, it divided into two bodies. The smaller one turned to capture some small artillery pieces, while the larger one, led by Conrad in person, went straight for the large siege guns, which they were successful in taking. Heinrich von Fürstenberg heard the noise and came to see what was happening. He got too close to the Swiss who dragged him from his horse and killed him. Thus at the very outset of the battle, the Imperial Army was deprived of its commander, but much of his army continued the fight without him. Conrad's group pushed on westward through the centre of the Swabian camp. These men were surprised, thrown into great confusion, and many, including the Welsch Guard, fled across the Birs stream.

Conrad and his men had shown great initiative, but the vanguard was too small to keep the Imperial Army in confusion for long. The Swabian Army began to form up in its order of battle, and the Welsch Guard returned from across the Birs to attack Conrad's forces. The Swiss vanguard was soon hard pressed and forced to fall back towards the forest. This contingent was only spared from slaughter by the skilful use of the pike and arquebus.[109]

The smaller part of the vanguard was able to take the enemy guns, but soon met stiff resistance as well. These men had to fight desperately to keep from being overwhelmed, but took heavy casualties in doing so. This group was saved from annihilation when the Swiss main body (*gewalthaufen*) of 3,000 men from Bern broke clear of the forest. The main force had advanced as rapidly as possible through the forest, but the dense undergrowth had slowed its progress. By the time it entered the field of battle, both sections of the vanguard were in grave danger, and the German Landsknechts, were forming into a large pike square. The smaller groups in the vanguard fell back to join the main formation, and these combined forces then marched on to meet the Germans.[110]

At that point, the battle became one of German infantry against Swiss infantry because the Swabian cavalry, and some of the Welsch Guard, withdrew from the fight. Many of them were raiding far away, and the 400 remaining were more interested in robbing the dead than in actually participating in the fighting. The artillery was also no factor in the battle even after the Swabian gunners returned after being chased from the field. They were unable to use their artillery pieces effectively because their larger weapons were set up to aim high in order to hit Dorneck and they were unable to train them on the Swiss. The Confederates were also forced to leave their cannon behind because they could not bring them through the forest to the field.

The Germans and the Swiss fought on the fields between Dornach and Arlesheim. The contest was costly and a prominence on the field of battle became known as 'Blood Hill.' For some time the two armies continued

---

109 Anshelm, *Berner-Chronik*, vol. 2, p.229.
110 Lenz, *Schwabenkrieg*, p.152.

their fight, the outnumbered Swiss making up in ferocity for what they lacked in manpower. No doubt, each side thrust with their pikes, while the men with halberds looked for any opening to rush forward and engage the enemy at closer quarters. The troops with firearms fired into the ranks of their enemy bringing noise and smoke to the battle and inflicting casualties at a distance from the close quarters battle. Both armies pushed back and forth against the other as the fighting swayed over the fields. Whenever one force made an advance into the other, there would be a rally by them, and the front would again become stable. Neither side was able to successfully break the other's ranks and the battle continued to rage fiercely, as the men on both sides became increasingly exhausted. It appeared that the battle would end as a stalemate if nothing changed.[111]

As nightfall was approaching, the battle was finally decided by the timely arrival of Swiss reinforcements from Lucerne and Zug. These troops entered the field of battle near Arlesheim, shouting and blowing horns, as they rushed to join the Swiss main body. With these fresh reinforcements, the Confederates staged their final attack. The sheer weight of the advance of the reinvigorated Swiss was too much for the exhausted Germans, and they broke and fled. The Confederates, incensed after their costly and difficulty victory, pursued their enemies as they attempted to flee across the Birs stream. The Swiss killed any of their adversaries when they could be caught, and in the ensuing darkness and confusion, the Confederates fell upon men of their own army, killing each other. When all of the men in the Imperial Army had fled across the Birs and total darkness had fallen, further pursuit became impossible. The exhausted Swiss laid down where they were and slept on the field.[112]

The conflict between the Swiss and the German mercenaries was bitter, and experienced soldiers testified to the ferocity of the action. Around 3,000 Germans and 500 Swiss died in the battle. The Confederates were buried, but their adversaries were left to rot. Imperial emissaries sought to recover the bodies of the fallen nobles, but the Swiss replied that they would have to remain with the peasants. Only the body of Heinrich von Fürstenberg was taken from the field, to the church at Arlesheim.[113]

The Swiss showed a great deal of concern for their wounded and for the families of the dead. The wounded were taken to nearby towns where they were cared for until they had fully recovered, or as far as they were going to recover in the case of the more seriously maimed. By common consent of the troops, all the booty taken in the battle was divided among the wounded and the widows and orphans of the dead.[114]

---

111 Rieter, 'Schwabenkrieg,' p.148 and Anshelm, *Berner-Chronik*, vol. 2, p.230.
112 Brennwald, *Schweizerchronik*, vol. 2, p.451.
113 'Hauptleute et cetera der Stadt Bern im Feld an Bern,' 24 July 1499 in *Aktenstücke*, pp.389–90 and Tatarinoff, *Beteiligung*, p.183.
114 Elgger, *Kriegswesen*, pp.172–3.

After the battle, the Swiss had an excellent opportunity to march into Alsace or into the Swabian lands, because that province was largely undefended, but the army showed little interest in such operations. It remained on the battlefield for six days and then returned home. Skirmishes took place in the area for several days, but the fighting soon died down. When Maximilian heard the news of the Swiss victory, he ended his military activities, which had become little more than an artillery exchange between the armies around Constance.[115]

To Die Free and Swiss: the Church at Thayngen 25 July 1499

Yet, before word of the Battle of Dornach caused many in the Imperial high command to lose confidence in victory, a highly significant raid on the Swiss village of Thayngen took place. In this case, a small Swiss garrison showed great courage and determination in a hopeless situation in the defence of the church at Thayngen, and their efforts became one of the most heroic actions of the entire war.

The Hegau area stretched from Schaffhausen, a close Swiss ally during the war, to the shores of Lake Constance, where many Swabian forces were stationed. To bring the war closer to its enemies and destroy their wealth and means of making war, troops from Schaffhausen and its Swiss allies had raided the Hegau three times during the war. The third expedition into the Hegau took place from 20 to 28 May 1499, and the three expeditions together had done considerable damage including the destruction of many fortresses, the plundering of the countryside, and the burning of numerous villages. Yet the Swiss had met with only limited success on the third expedition. They marched as far as the town of Stockach, Germany, but were unable to take the fortress which was defended by a garrison of 800 capable German soldiers. Swiss prisoners stated that the attacking Confederate force numbered 9,000 men but that they were suffering a great deal from hunger. Among them were 2,000 boys and women dressed as men.[116] This incident, in which persons usually considered non-combatants were 'deployed', illustrated the fact that the Swiss had strained their resources and were using desperate measures on operations late in the war.

The German cavalry stationed in the Hegau area and near Constance 'swore bloody revenge' against the Swiss, and got their opportunity to strike back during a raid on 25 July 1499. A number of important leaders led the raid, including the Margraf von Baden and Brandenburg, Herzog Alexander von Bayern and Ulrich von Württemberg. The infamous Ytelhans Stoffler,

---

115 Brennwald, *Schweizerchronik*, vol. 2, p.455
116 'Ulrich Strauss zu Ueberlingen an Nördlingen,' 30 May 1499, *Urkunden zur Geschichte des Schwäbischen Bundes*, vol. 1, p.341.

THE SWABIAN WAR OF 1499

The Victory Against France, woodcut based on a drawing by Hans Springinklee, showing a siege, with gun lines before the fortifications and infantry deployed on the edge of the army's camp. (Metropolitan Museum of Art, Harris Brisbane Dick Fund, 1928)

known as 'the evil' (*der Böse*) was almost certainly there, and Willibald Pirkheimer, the humanist and historian, was one of the leaders from Nuremberg. Additionally, many troops came from the cities and towns of Swabia and the Hegau region. In an obvious attempt to move rapidly, the cavalry initially left their infantry behind. The foot soldiers stood in combat formation on a flat area just a few kilometres east of Thayngen near the villages of Bietingen and Gottmadingen, where they awaited orders to advance. The Imperial forces struck shortly after midnight on the night of 24/25 July, meaning they had marched for several hours through the darkness with little, if any, sleep after sunset. They took and burnt 11 villages in all, and killed as many peasants as they could find or catch.

Walls and fences were common features in towns, villages, and the countryside during the Middle Ages, and they made a difference in the areas of active campaigning during the war. These barriers were made of wood or stone, and were used to mark territory and to provide some protection against thieves and wild animals. In times of conflict, these obstacles helped protect communities from raids and attacks. The village of Thayngen was in a dangerous location, near enemy communities and garrisons, and its inhabitants had every reason to fear attacks or retaliations for raids. At the time of the raid on Thayngen, the war had been waged for some months, giving the people of the town ample opportunity to improve their defences by strengthening them with additional fortifications and entrenchments.

While the town was fortified by the time of the raid, one of the most defensible positions in the village was the community church. During the Middle Ages, houses of worship frequently had walls around them to give some separation between holy spaces inside the enclosure and the common areas outside. Additionally, the walls frequently provided some protection from possible incursions. These barriers were also meant to protect the graveyards, often located on the site, and also the approaches to the church. The churches were commonly constructed of stone to demonstrate permanence and strength. Because of the price and technical aspects of stone construction for rafters and roofs, these were commonly built of wood, meaning that they were vulnerable to fire. The churches themselves were usually composed of two main components: the nave or main chapel was a place for the congregation to sit during prayer or services, and the tower was also frequently a part of the building. The tower was often designed to accommodate a bell to be used to inform the congregation of church and community functions.

In times of war, the sound of the bell was often used to warn of attacks or to call men to arms. Such structures often towered above the countryside which made good watch posts as well as excellent defensive positions. The churchyard at Thayngen was surrounded with trenches, and the house of worship had a 'good, large tower' with high and thick walls and with openings from which defenders could fire weapons.[117] An eyewitness, Willibald Pirckheimer, further described the church at Thayngen as 'very large' with an 'extremely well-fortified tower.' The fact that Thayngen was located on a border area meant that the church and tower could have been constructed at least partially with defence in mind.

Even though the initial attack on the town took place during the night, some of the people in the community had some warning and enough time to flee into the nearby forests and vineyards taking their cattle with them. The raiding party brought a number of artillery pieces with them, and they used the cannon 'small and large' to bombard the community. When the cavalry pushed over the fences and other barriers into the hamlet, some men of the village ran to the strongly-protected churchyard, from which they could only watch helplessly as the village was pounded by artillery, then burnt, and plundered. These cavalry soon turned their attention to the men behind the walled churchyard, and the siege began.

The fight for the village and the church took all day, lasting 15 to 20 hours. The Swiss position was too strong to be taken directly by a cavalry attack, so the cavalry dismounted to carry the fight to their enemy on foot. They also wanted to take the position before the infantry came up and participated in the attack because they thought it a disgrace to call on the lower classes to help with the assault of the position. The dismounted cavalry then advanced against the defenders behind the churchyard walls. But the Swiss were too few in number, only 30 or 33, to hold the position long, and soon fell back into the church and tower where the fighting intensified.

The Swiss ran into the church, barricaded the doors, and took up positions in the chapel and tower where they continued to resist by shooting arrows and bullets, and throwing stones from loopholes or arrow slits in the church and tower. At that point, the cavalry attack on the church made little military sense. The garrison in the church was too small and too isolated to interfere with the destruction and plundering of the village, and

---

117 Lenz, *Schwabenkrieg*, p.127.

the time and resources wasted on the attack could have been better used elsewhere; the Imperial forces could have simply ignored the church and carried on with other aspects of the raid. Perhaps the cavalry felt that they needed to take the church to show their courage and ferocity and to punish the defenders, but pure hatred for the Swiss was no doubt a factor as well. This act of vengeance proved to be a costly mistake.

A young noble, Götz von Berlichingen, only 19-years old and still a squire at the time, was with the Imperial raid on Thayngen. Later known as 'Götz of the Iron Hand,' because he wore an artificial right hand after this appendage was shot off in 1504, he was to be immortalised in a play by the German poet, Johann Wolfgang von Goethe. Late in life, Berlichingen wrote an important autobiography in which he described the fight for the church at Thayngen. 'A few Swiss sat in the church tower of the village and defended themselves.' The Imperial forces then called upon the men in the church to surrender. In one of the most defiant gestures of the entire war, the defenders stated that, 'they did not want to surrender.' Instead, they said they, 'would rather die as pious Confederates.' In some versions, the account reads, 'They said they would rather die as brave Confederates' (*Als wie fromme [tapfere] Eydsgnossen*). [118] In fact, either or both versions might be accurate, yet the precise wording is unimportant because Swiss defiance was clear in either case, and the defenders were definitely willing to give their lives rather than capitulate.

Swiss returning from a raid into Swabian territory, print by Evert van Muuden (Author's collection)

Actually, yielding to a superior force might have been a viable option for the men in the church, and the treatment of prisoners during the war was not always poor. Nobles and the wealthy were valued by their captors because they could be ransomed, and their families would often pay large sums to assure their timely release, but the peasants in the church were worth much less – if anything at all. However prisoners from the lower classes were often exchanged during the war, and a swift release was a reasonable expectation. Even if they

---

118 Gözens von Berlichingen, *Lebens Beschreibung* (Nürnberg: Adam Jonathan Fellsecker, 1731), p.41.

were held in captivity any length of time, the Swiss still had a good chance of survival.

Of course, the greatest fear of surrendering troops was that they would be killed when they capitulated, but the terms of submission during the war were often negotiated, and the defenders would have required assurances that their lives would be spared. At times, captives were unmolested, released on the spot, and even allowed to leave carrying what valuables they could with them. No doubt, such pledges were not always honoured, but the chances of survival were much better when surrendering under terms than with the near certainty of death in the church. The defence of the church made little sense militarily because it had little strategic value. If the church were held or not, the village would still be plundered and burnt. The only real reasons for defending the church were to show the defenders' courage and to defy an invading foe; the Swiss clearly thought risking their lives in a near hopeless situation was worth the price.

Melchior Süzel, a nobleman from the area, tried to drive the defenders from the building, but a Swiss hit him in the face with a stone, and the defenders soon threw the heavy cavalry back with many 'bloody heads.' The men in the tower not only threw stones at their attackers, but also used their arquebuses to great effect. Even though the arquebus was notoriously inaccurate, the marksmen in the church used it to kill a number of their attackers, both mounted and on foot. Berlichingen took part in the fight for the church, and when the defenders shot his horse, he ran to the church with the other men on foot and armed himself with a spear because he had left his sword on his mount's saddle. The young squire was standing next to a gunsmith, Master Jacob, 'a small very thin man,' when the latter was hit. The bullet went through Master Jacob and struck the soldier behind him who was only wearing simple clothing, and had no armour for protection. Jacob survived his wound, but the man behind him died.

The Swiss had locked and barricaded the doors, so the Imperial forces used battering rams to smash in the portals of the church, but the defenders still defended the position with 'extreme courage.' Once inside the Germans plundered the church, but also tried to burn out or smoke out the defenders. They placed 'grain, hay, wood, straw and other such materials that would burn' in the church and set everything on fire, but this effort was largely ineffective, and the Swiss continued to resist. But the defenders' position continued to be precarious if not completely hopeless.

Finally, Sebaldus Spät and other men brought one or two barrels of gunpowder to incinerate those inside once the explosive material had been ignited.[119] The Germans had either dug underneath the tower or used artillery to pound a hole in the tower, and they placed the barrels of gunpowder in it, where they ignited it. After he described the initial explosion under the tower, Berlichingen stated that a Swiss soldier 'fell'

---

119 Lenz, *Schwabenkrieg*, p.128.

THE SWABIAN WAR OF 1499

from the tower – the man could have jumped or been blown out by the detonation – whatever the case he held a small boy, 'a little boy with yellow hair' in his arms.[120] The man was killed but the child walked, or toddled, away unhurt. One of the cavalry picked up the small boy, but Berlichingen had no knowledge of what happened to the child afterwards because he never saw it again.

The igniting of the powder was poorly timed because some Germans were still in the church at that time. It seemed they had delayed leaving the building because they wanted more time to plunder the interior. The exploding powder overtook them, and they must have suffered miserably. Berlichingen had no further knowledge of these men, and he did not know if they lived or died but none of them ran out of the building. As Berlichingen and others hurried out of the building, they formed into battle order waiting for the Swiss to rush out, but no one came, so the Germans marched away. If any of the defenders were still alive after the powder explosion, they preferred a fiery death to surrender.

Willibald Pirckheimer was another eyewitness to the attack on Thayngen, and he gave a slightly different account of the destruction of the church tower. According to Pirckheimer, the barrels of gunpowder were ignited 'with monstrous force' which 'blew the defenders into the air just as if [they were] a swarm of birds [which] had taken flight from the same place so that most of them fell to the earth dead.'[121] The explosion was so terrific that it completely destroyed the tower and 'no stone was left near another.' The cost in casualties for the Imperial forces to take Thayngen were high, and reportedly, from 80 men to as many as 200 men died in the attempt to take the church and tower, which was a heavy cost in comparison to the little that they accomplished.

Helmet c. 1490-1500. The ventilation holes in the visor forming an X-shape or saltire allude to the Cross of St Andrew, a Burgundian emblem that was adopted by the Habsburgs and used as an insignia by Imperial troops. (Metropolitan Museum of Art, Bashford Dean Memorial Collection, Bequest of Bashford Dean, 1928)

The news of the attack on Thayngen had reached Schaffhausen early in the day, and observers at that town could clearly see the smoke from the burning village which was about 10 kilometres away. The military leaders had to assess the situation and decide on a course of action before anything could be done, but a force reported to be 800 men were soon on the march towards Thayngen. By the time this force arrived, the Imperial troops had already accomplished their goals in the raid, and they did not want to test their courage in an unnecessary battle, and they withdrew after sunset.

---

120 Lenz, *Schwabenkrieg*, p.128.
121 Pirckheimer, *Schweizerkrieg*, p.190, German.

The action at Thayngen took place three days after the Battle of Dornach, which proved to be the decisive action of the war. The news of that engagement had yet to reach the Imperial troops engaged in the raid on Thayngen, and that information could have delayed or even cancelled the incursion into the village. After the Battle of Dornach, many important Imperial leaders of the war quickly recognised that further efforts would be fruitless. If this had been the same opinion of the leaders of the raid, it might have never taken place.

The defence of the church and tower of Thayngen was one of the most impressive feats of arms in the Swabian War. Hopelessly outnumbered, the garrison at Thayngen defended their position for hours, and by a skilful defence, caused heavy casualties on the Imperial forces. In several respects, the defence of Thayngen is comparable with the Battle of St Jakob an der Birs in 1444. In that engagement, a small Swiss force of about 1,300 men attacked a French army of at least 20,000. The Swiss retreated to a walled hospital where they held off attacks for many hours, inflicting heavy casualties on their enemies. Only a few Swiss survived the onslaught to escape when darkness fell. In each of these instances, the Swiss fought to the death rather than surrender.[122]

The End of a Senseless War

After the Battle of Dornach, the war effort by The Empire almost collapsed because continued fighting was considered to be fruitless. Both sides were exhausted, and the Swiss similarly showed little interest in further battles and raids. Military activity dropped off until early in August, when there was hardly any fighting at all. Negotiations were held in Basel, and on 22 September 1499, the Peace of Basel was signed. Despite the huge loss of life, the great human suffering, and the extensive physical destruction caused by the war, little had changed. No territory changed hands, the alliance system in the areas of Grisons remained in place, and the areas subject to the Habsburgs retained their former relations. According to the Peace, Maximilian recognised he had no further authority to tax or to put courts over the Swiss Confederation, which was a condition that had largely existed before the war.[123] In reality, the Swiss had become independent even though they retained nominal attachment to the Holy Roman Empire until the Treaty of Westphalia in 1648. Perhaps the largest single change brought by the war was not in the social and political areas but in demonstrating that the Swabian infantry was very much on the ascendancy.

---

122 Kurz, *Schweizerschlachten*, pp.[69]–84.
123 Kurz, *Schweizerschlachten*, p.178.

The Decline of the Swiss Military

There were many weaknesses in the Swiss military at the end of the fifteenth century that contributed to its decline as the dominant infantry in the coming decades. Warfare became more complex, foreign infantry was greatly improved, artillery became a greater factor in combat, and the Swiss themselves suffered from a weakening of discipline, morale, and integrity.

By the beginning of the sixteenth century, other armies had developed into forces with artillery, disciplined infantry, and tactically flexible cavalry. They also began to put in place more ingeniously prepared positions for defence with trenches and other obstacles. All of these developments introduced new factors into the complexity of warfare. Armies had greater opportunities to employ new methods of fighting rather than the simple cavalry attack that had been common on many battlefields in the fourteenth and fifteenth centuries. Rather than adopting more flexibility to be more effective in battle, the Swiss clung to their old tactics of advancing in squares, which soon proved to be outmoded. The Confederates had shown some adaptability in the Swabian War, but following that conflict, the Swiss turned back to traditional ways of fighting rather than changing to meet the times.

The first foreign infantry to challenge the Swiss seriously were the Swabian Landsknechts (literally, 'servants of the land'). These two infantries met in a number of engagements first in the Swabian War and on other occasions later in the early sixteenth century, the most notable of which was the Battle of Bicocca in 1522. The engagements in the Swabian War were bitter fights that were fiercely contested, and as at the Battle of Dornach in 1499, it was not definite that the Swiss were superior to the German mercenaries. Beginning in 1500, the most effective infantry used against the Swiss were the Spanish infantry of Consalvo de Cordova which had adopted many of the tactics of the ancient Romans in the wars in Northern Italy. Using sword and shield, the Spanish were able to ward off the Swiss pikes in numerous engagements. Having no shield to deflect the slashing and thrusting Spanish, the disadvantaged Confederates were forced to discard their longer weapons to use their swords.[124]

Artillery and the arquebus had become important factors in combat, and these two weapons increasingly killed more men in battle.[125] The Swiss pike square was the easiest possible infantry formation at which to fire cannon, and the improvements in powder and munitions made artillery-fire all the more effective. The tactics that Heinrich Wolleb used at the Battle of Franstanz in 1499 of falling down before enemy fire to make smaller targets was unheard of after the Swabian War, meaning that the Swiss would frequently stand to face enemy fire. This was a costly mistake because falling to the ground

---

124 Oman, *Art of War*, vol. 2, pp.275–276.
125 Kurz, *Schweizerschlachten*, pp.144–145.

was the best way to reduce casualties under heavy fire, and the great Swiss bravery was often misplaced. Starting in the early sixteenth century, such courage proved to be more costly than effective.[126]

The largest single factor in the Swiss decline was the lack of discipline and unity in battle. This was caused, to a great extent, by a major change taking place in Swiss society early in the sixteenth century. More and more, mercenary service had become a major source of wealth in the Confederation, and large sums of money came in the form of bribes and payments. Corruption at all levels became a fact, and often payoffs to canton and civic officials were the major inducement to many official actions. This malfeasance went from the leaders who received bribes to the rank and file who got payments for military service. The once proud Swiss military became greedy and lost the sense of duty which had been common in earlier times.[127]

The problem of corruption was not alleviated even when the Swiss defeats during the first 25 years of the sixteenth century made soldiers harder to procure. This difficulty in getting troops occurred because the casualties diminished the available manpower, and young men were not as eager to enlist when greater dangers were involved. Yet because of the difficulty in obtaining soldiers, the fees for their services went up, perpetuating a high level of corruption for decades to come.[128]

The Swiss War, woodcut based on a drawing by Wolf Traut. (Metropolitan Museum of Art, Harris Brisbane Dick Fund, 1928)

The Confederation became plagued with difficulties. The number of men going into military service meant that agriculture became neglected by the most vigorous section of the population, and morals became increasingly lax. The change appears to have been most rapid after 1480 since from this time laws regulating standards of behaviour became more frequent. By 1503, Swiss conduct and character had become objects of scorn for both citizen and foreigner alike. As in most instances of legislated morality, these statutes regulating conduct proved difficult to enforce,

---

126 Gessler, *Geschützwesen*, p.56.
127 Vincent, *Switzerland*, p.12.
128 Vincent, *Switzerland*, p.15.

especially when the government officials who passed the laws were notably corrupt themselves.[129]

This decline in ethical conduct affected every facet of the military. Leaders became unwilling to lead unless they received more pay than the other troops, and soldiers themselves began to lack discipline and unity in battle. These men no longer made such great efforts, and their effectiveness wavered.[130] The Battle of Novara in 1513 was the last victory won by the Swiss using their traditional tactics. At the Battle of Marignano in 1515, the Confederate attacking columns disobeyed orders and failed to advance on the enemy's flank. Instead, they moved head on against the fortified enemy position. As a result, the Swiss were slaughtered and faced their first major defeat on the battlefield in more than a half century. At the Battle of Bicocca in 1522, the Confederates made no pretence of a flank attack and moved directly on the trenches manned by the Landsknechts. As a result, the Swiss suffered another major defeat which gave the Germans revenge on the Confederates for numerous actions during the Swabian War.

After the Battle of Bicocca, the Confederates fell from their position as being considered as the most formidable soldiers of the age. Surprisingly though, much of Swiss reputation survived their great defeats. Although their tactics were clearly outmoded and the Confederates themselves held their military in derision, they were still among the most sought-after soldiers in Europe. France, ever respectful of the Swiss military, always fielded a large contingent of Swiss mercenaries within its armies throughout the mid-sixteenth century. Clearly, many European states had been so respectful of the Swiss military that its failures were put aside, and the belief in Swiss abilities persisted long after their effectiveness in battle was put in question.

---

129 Anshelm, *Berner-Chronik*, vol. 2, p.464 and Vincent, *Switzerland*, pp.23–29.
130 Elgger, *Kriegswesen*, p.197.

6

Conclusion

The Swabian War was one of Maximilian's failures in his attempt to unify the Holy Roman Empire under the control of the Habsburgs. While the conflict did not spell the end of his efforts at unification, it was a major setback. Militarily, the war was very significant: in it, Europe witnessed the first clashes between two genuine tactical infantry since the era of Ancient Rome. Infantry were not to entirely replace cavalry for centuries, but the era of cavalry supported by weak and ineffective foot soldiers was over.

Despite the victorious outcomes of the major engagements in the Swabian War, the Confederates had been unable to show an overwhelming superiority over their enemies. Both the Battle of Calven and of Dornach had been costly and closely-contested affairs which left open the question of the continuing dominance of the Swiss. In the war, the Swabian Landsknechts proved themselves to be a formidable force, but the Swiss remained undefeated and still at the height of their prestige. The resolution of the contest for superiority between the Swiss and the German mercenaries was not settled in the Swabian War and would not be decided until the severe Swiss defeat at the Battle of Bicocca in 1522.

The Swiss Confederation fought the Swabian War with 10 official members. Because the Confederation had shown itself to be viable and able to protect its interests, other states joined, and it soon had 13 members. Yet, the most important result of the Swabian War for Swiss history could not be conceived of at the time. This conflict was to represent the last major attempt by a foreign power to invade the Confederation for nearly three centuries. A major reason for this situation was the respect in which the Swiss military was held. Over the previous two centuries, time and again, it had shown its superiority over virtually all forces sent to meet it. This impressive feat meant that the Confederates could decide their own destiny largely free from the domination of foreign powers. The Swiss national development owed much to the military, but this advance would have been impossible without the significant social developments which made that martial institution possible.

Colour Plates Commentary

(by Stephen Ede-Borrett)

Plate A. Swiss Pikeman
The doublet is of a padded 'jacket' style which offered some protection on its own but he has then added a modern two-piece breastplate (and backplate, not visible here) with lames below in place of longer tassets, and additional protection at the armpits. He has painted a fairly crude white cross across his armour and also displays the Confederation's cross on the thigh of his hose. Like the League standard bearer he almost certainly has a steel cap underneath his ostentatious headwear, which itself shows he is not a poor peasant.

Plate B. Swiss Arquebusier/handgunner
His hose shows the St George's Cross of the Confederation – as ordered to be worn by all soldiers. The weapon still has elements of the earlier primitive handguns but is recognisable as an early arquebus. The first piece of armour that any soldiers aimed to acquire was a helmet (you rarely recover from a serious head wound) and this man is wearing a particularly fine visored sallet – perhaps the spoils of previous service.

Plate C. Swiss Hornblower, Canton of Zurich
The hornblower is dressed in the blue (usually shown as this shade of sky-blue) and white of the colours of the Canton's Arms (per bend azure and argent), an affectation fairly common among both hornblowers and ensigns of all cantons. Despite the usual depictions it would be customary for such men to carry some sort of polearm to allow them to defend themselves even if not in the attack – in this case the individual carries a form of bill.

Plate D. Swabian League Master Gunner
His clothing is typical of that for a professional man of the period. Such 'Master Gunners' needed to be both gunners and mathematicians and, if they had a reputation, were much sought after and could serve almost anywhere across the Continent.

COLOUR PLATES COMMENTARY

Plate E. Swabian League Landsknecht Pikeman
His appearance is an amalgam copied from a number of woodcuts of the period. Whether the bare legs was an affectation for battle or whether it reflected day to day appearance is unknown. He is shown without armour but could have a back and breast with tassets and may have a 'secrete' under his cap.

Plate F. Swabian League standard bearer
Very fashionably, and somewhat expensively, dressed he sports the Habsburg Cross of St Andrew both on the shoulder of his doublet and etched across his breastplate.

Plate G. The flags shown are, clockwise from top left: the banner of the Canton of Bern, the Standard of a company of Swiss arquebusiers, the Standard of Imperial cavalry of Maximilian I and the Standard of the Swabian League.

Plate H. The Battle of Dornach (Schlacht bei Dorneck)
Details of a near-contemporary woodcut (the colouring may be contemporary with the woodcut).
As is common with such illustrations, several phases of the battle are shown simultaneously. The main battle is depicted in the centre, while at the bottom, the pursuit and slaughter of the defeated at the River Birs are illustrated. The woodcut excellently portrays both Swiss and Imperial troops at the battle, although many of the heavy 'gendarme-like' cavalry may have already abandoned lower leg armour by 1499. Notably, the Swiss pike are shown in front of those with shorter polearms, although these are present in substantial numbers. The depiction of both heavier and lighter field cannon is also well done. The various Swiss and Imperial flags appear to be accurate, and the correctness of their coloring suggests that the hues shown for the troops may also be a close approximation of their appearance at the time.
(Public Domain via Marco Zanoli/Wikipedia Commons)

Bibliography

Primary Sources

Anonymous, *Amtliche Sammlung der ältern Eidgenössischen Abschiede*, 8 volumes. (Lucerne: Wener'sche Buchdruckerei, 1858–1874) [Includes 458 official statements from the Swiss Federal Diet relating to the Swabian War]

Anonymous, 'Acta des Tyroler-Kriegs,' *Rätia Geschichtsforschende Gesellschaft von Graubünden,* 4 (1869): 111–149

Anonymous (Placid Bütler ed.), *Wiler Chronik des Schwabenkriegs* (St Gallen: Fehr, 1914)

Anshelm, Valerius, *Die Berner-Chronik* 6 volumes. (Bern: K. J. Wyss, 1886)

Berlichingen, Gözens von, *Lebens Beschreibung* (Nürnberg: Adam Jonathan Fellsecker, 1731) Brennwald, Heinrich, *Schweizerchronik,* 2 volumes. (Basel: Basler Buch-und Antiquariatshandlung, 1910)

Büchi, Albert (ed.), *Aktenstücke zur Geschichte des Schwabenkrieges nebst einer Freiburger Chronik über die Ereignisse von 1499*, (Basel: Basler Buch-und Antiquariatshandlung, 1901) [Includes 710 documents relating to the Swabian War]

Crussi, Martin, *Schwäbischer Chronik* (Franckfurt: Metzler und Erhard, 1733)

Edlibach, Gerold, *Chronik* (Zürich: Meyer und Zeller, 1847)

Etterlin, Peterman, *Kronica von der loblichen Eidgnoschaft* (Basel: Eckenstein, 1752)

Feer, Ludwig, 'Ettliche Chronickwürdige sachen durch Ludwig Feeren der Zytt Stattschryber zu Lucerne beschrieben, Anno 1499,' *Der Geschichtsfreund* (1845), vol. 2, pp.133–148

Haffner, Anton, *Chronica* (Solothurn: Franz Xaver Zepfel, 1849)

Hug, Heinrich, *Villinger Chronik von 1495 bis 1533* (Tübingen: Literarischer Verein Stuttgart, 1883)

Jecklin, C. and F. (eds.), *Der Anteil Graubündens am Schwabenkrieg* (Davos: E. Ricter'sche Buchdruckerei, 1899). [includes excerpts from relevant primary sources and 260 messages and letters relating to the war]

Klüpfel, K. (ed.), *Urkunden zur Geschichte des Schwäbischen Bundes (1488–1533)*, 2 vols (Stuttgart: literarischer Verein, 1846) [includes 151 official documents relating to the Swabian War]

Lemnius, Simon, (Placidus Plattner, ed.) *Die Raeteis: Schweizerisch-Deutcher Kreieg von 1499* (Chur: Sprecher & Plattner, 1874)

Lenz, Johann, *Der Schwabenkrieg* (Zürich: Orell Füssli, 1849)

[Nauclerus, Johannes], *Chronicon Iohannes Naucleri* (Coloniae [Cologne]: No publisher, 1564), vol. 2

Oechsli, Wilhelm, (ed.), *Quellenbuch zur Schweizergeschichte* (Zürich: Schultheß, 1918) [Includes excerpts from nine primary sources related to the Swabian War]

[Pirckheimer, Willibald], *Bilibald Pirkheimers Schweizerkrieg und Ehrenhandel mit seinen Feinden zu Nürnberg nebst Biographie und kritischem Schriftenverzeichnis durch Ernst Münch*, (Basel: Schweighauser'schen Buchhandlung, 1826). Münch's German translation of the Latin original is found on pp.72–206. The section on the Swabian War starts on page 117

[Pirckheimer, Willibald], Karl Rück, (ed.), *Wilibald Pirckheimers Schweizerkrieg: nach Pirckheimers Autographum im Britischen Museum*, (München: K. Akademie, 1895). Original Latin text

Schilling, Diebold, (Gustav Tobler, ed.) *Die Berner-Chronik 1468–1484*. 2 vols (Bern: K. J. Wyss, 1897–1901)

Schilling, Diebold, *Die Schweizer Bilderchonik des Lucerners Diebold Schilling 1513* (Lucerne: Faksimilie Verlag, 1981)

Schradin, Nicolaus, 'Der Schwabenkrieg vom J. 1499 besungen in teutschen Reimen durch Nicolaus Schradin, Schreiber zu Lucern 1500,' *Der Geschichtsfreund* 4 (1847), pp.3–66

Tatarinoff, Eugen (ed.), *ie Beteiligung Solothurn am Schwabenkriege bis zur Schlacht bei Dornach 22. July 1499* (Solothurn: A. Luety, 1899) [includes 172 official documents relating to the siege of Dorneck and the Battle of Dornach]

Secondary Sources

Brady, Thomas A. *Turning Swiss: Cities and Empire, 1450-1550* (New York: Cambridge University Press, 1985)

Caviezel, M., *Die Calvenschlacht: eine Denkschritft an das Bündnervolk* (Franken: Simon Tanner, 1899)

Delbrück, Hans, *Geschichte der Kriegskunst im Rahmen der politischen Geschichte*, vol. 3 (Berlin: Stilke, 1923)

Delbrück, Hans (Walter J. Renfroe, Jr, trans.), *History of the Art of War* vol. 3 *Medieval Warfare* (Lincoln: University of Nebraska Press, 1990)

Dürr, Emil, 'Die Politik der Eidgenossen im XIV und XV Jahrhundert,' *Schweizer Kriegsgeschichte* 4 (1933), pp.460–503

BIBLIOGRAPHY

Elgger, Carl von, *Kriegswesen und Kriegskunst der Schweizerischen Eidgenossen im XIV, XV und XVI Jahrhundert* (Lucerne: Militärisches Verlagsbureau, 1873)

Feger, Otto, 'Probleme der Kriegsgefangenschaft im Schwabenkrieg,' *Zeitschrift für Schweizerishche Geschichte* 30 (1950), pp.595–601

Frauenholz, Eugen von, *Das Heerwesen der Schweizer Eidgenossenschaft* (München: Beck, 1936)

Frey, Emil, *Die Kriegstaten der Schweizer dem Volk erzält* (Neuenburg: F. Bahn, 1904)

Gessler, Edward A., *Das Schweizerishche Geschützwesen zur Zeit des Schwabenkriegs, 1499* (Zürich: Kommissionsverlag, 1927)

Gessler, Edward A., 'Die Waffenübungen der Jungend in der alten Eidgenossenschaft mit besoderer Berücksichtigung Zürichs,' *Zürich Taschenbuch* 23 (1923), pp.195–220

Hadron, Walther, 'Neues zur Laupenschlacht,' *Blätter für bernischen Geschichte, Kunst und Altertumskunde* 3 Jahrgang 2 Heft (May 1907), pp.120–125

Häne, Johannes, 'Die Kriegsbereitschaft der alten Eidgnossen,' *Schweizer Kriegsgeschichte* 3 (1915), pp 5–33

Hare, Christopher, *Maximilian the Dreamer: Holy Roman Emperor, 1459–1519* (New York: Charles Scribner's Sons, 1913)

Hess, Otto, *Die Fremden Büchsenmeister und Söldner in den Diensten: Der Eidgen-Orte bis 1516* (Dietikon: J. G. Hunndel-Horner, 1919)

Hobohm, Martin, *Machiavellis Renaissance der Kriegskunst* (Berlin: Karl Curtius, 1913)

Hug, Lina and Richard Stead, *Switzerland* (New York: G.P. Putnam's Sons, 1920)

Jäger, Albert, 'Der Engadeiner Krieg im 1499, mit Urkunden,' *Neue Zeitschrift des Ferdinandeums für Tyrol und Vorarlberg*, vol. 4 (1838), pp.1–227

Kurz, Hans Rudolf, *Schweizerschlachten* (Bern: Francke, 1962)

Laffont, Robert, *The Ancient Art of Warfare*, 2 vols. (Paris: Robert Laffont, 1966)

Theodor von Liebenau, *Die Schlacht bei Sempach: Gedenkbuch zur fünften Säcularfeier* (Lucerne: Prell, 1886)

Luginbühl, Rudolf, 'Das Gefecht auf dem Bruderholz,' *Basler Jahrbuch* (1904), pp.174–205

Maurer, Helmut, *Schweizer und Schwaben: Ihre Begegnung und Ihr Auseinanderleben am Bodensee in Spätmittelater* (Konstanz: Universitätsverlag, 1983)

Müller, Josef, 'Heini Wolleb: Hauptmann der Urner, Held zu Frastenz im Schwabenkrieger gefallen den 20. April 1499 daselbst' *Historisches Neujahrsblatt* (1898), pp.[45]–69

Niederhäuser, Peter (ed.), *Vom 'Freiheitskrieg' zum Geschichtsmythos: 500 Jahre Schweizer – oder Schwabenkrieg* (Zürich: Chronos, 2000)

Oman, Charles, *A History of the Art of War in the Middle Ages* vol. 2 1278–1485 (New York: Franklin, 1924)

Oman, Charles, *A History of the Art of War in the Sixteenth Century* (London: Methuen, 1937)

Padrutt, Christian, *Staat und Krieg im alten Bünden* (Zürich: Fretz und Wasmuth, 1965)

Rieter, Fritz, 'Der Schwabenkrieg vor 450 Jahren,' *Schweizer Monatshefte* 29 (June 1949), pp.129–150

Schaufelberger, Walter, *Die alte Schweizer und sein Kreig: Studien zur Kreigführung vornehmlich in 15. Jahrhundert* (Zürich: Europa, 1952)

'Die Schlacht bei Franstanz 1499,' *Rheticus: Vierteljahresschrift der Rheticus-Gesellschaft* Jahrgang 21 (1999) Heft 2, pp.[93]–198

Scott, Tom, *The Swiss and their Neighbours, 1460-1560: Between Accommodation and Aggression* (Oxford: Oxford University Press, 2017)

Sennhauser, Albert, *Hauptmann und Führung in Schweizerkrieg des Mittelalters* (Zürich: Fretz und Wasmuth, 1965)

Sidler, P. Wilhelm, *Die Schlacht am Morgarten* (Zürich: Orell Füssli, 1910)

Ulmann, Heinrich, *Kaiser Maxiliain I: Auf urkunlicher Grundlage Dargestellt* 2 vols (Stuttgart: Gotta, 1884)

Various, *Calven 1499-1999: Vorträge der Wissenschaftlichen Tagung im Rathaus Glurns vom 8. Bis 11. September 1999* (Lana: Tappeiner, 2001)

Vincent, John Martin, *Switzerland at the Beginning of the Sixteenth Century Sixteenth Century* (Baltimore: Johns Hopkins Press, 1904)

Winkler, Albert, 'The Battle of Morgarten: an Essential Incident in the Founding of the Swiss State,' *Swiss American Historical Society Review*, volume 44, no.3, November 2008 (Provo: BYU Scholars Archive 2010), pp.3–25

Winkler, Albert, 'The Battle of Murten: The Invasion of Charles the Bold and the Survival of the Swiss States,' *Swiss American Historical Society Review* volume 46, no.1, February 2010 (Provo: BYU Scholars Archive 2010), pp.8–34

Winzeler, Johannes, *Geschichte von Thayngen* (Thayngen: Karl Augustin, 1963)

About the author

Albert Winkler has three Masters' Degrees and a Ph.D. in Medieval Warfare, and his dissertation dealt with the Swiss military in the Middle Ages. He has published nearly sixty books and articles, almost all dealing with military history, and he has twice been given the prestigious best article of the year award from the *Utah Historical Quarterly*. He is currently a history instructor at Utah Valley University, and he was voted teacher of the year in 2010 by over six hundred students at that institution.

About the Artist

Giorgio Albertini was born in 1968 in Milan where he still lives. After studying Medieval History at the University of Milan, he become involved in archaeology and has been involved in several excavations for European institutions. He was responsible for the graphic depiction of archaeological sites and finds. He also works as a historical and scientific illustrator for many institutions, museums, and magazines such as *National Geographic Magazine*, *BBC History*, and *Medieval Warfare*. He has always been interested in military history and is one of the founders of *Focus Wars* magazine.

Other titles in the From Retinue to Regiment series:

No 1 *Richard III and the Battle of Bosworth* Mike Ingram

No 2 *Tanaka 1587: Japan's Greatest Unknown Samurai Battle* Stephen Turnbull

No 3 *The Army of the Swabian League 1525* Doug Miller

No 4 *The Italian Wars Volume 1: The Expedition of Charles VIII into Italy and the Battle of Fornovo* Massimo Predonzani & Alberici Vincenzo, translated by Irene Maccolini

No 5 *The Commotion Time: Tudor Rebellion in the West, 1549* E.T. Fox

No 6 *The Italian Wars Volume 2: Agnadello 1509, Ravenna 1512, Marignano 1515* Massimo Predonzani & Alberici Vincenzo, translated by Rachele Tiso

No 7 *The Tudor Arte of Warre Volume 1: The Conduct of War from Henry VII to Mary I, 1485-1558* Jonathan Davies

No 8 *The Ethiopian-Adal War 1529-1543: The Conquest of Abyssinia* Jeffrey M. Shaw

No 9 *The Ōnin War: A Turning Point in Samurai History* Stephen Turnbull

No 10 *One Faith, One Law, One King: French Armies of the Wars of Religion 1562–1598* T J O'Brien de Clare

No 11 *The Italian Wars Volume 3: Francis I and the Battle of Pavia 1525* Massimo Predonzani & Alberici Vincenzo

No 12 *On the Borderlands of Great Empires: Transylvanian Armies 1541-1613* Florin Nicolae Ardelean

No 14 *The Art of Shooting Great Ordnance: A History of the Development, Manufacture and Use of Artillery, 1494–1628* Jonathan Davies

No 15 *The Italian Wars Volume 4: The Battle of Ceresole 1544 - The Crushing Defeat of the Imperial Army* Massimo Predonzani & Simon Miller

No 16 *The Men of Warre: The Clothes, Weapons and Accoutrements of the Scots at War 1460–1600* Jenn Scott

No 17 *The German Peasants' War 1524–26* Douglas Miller

No 18 *The Tudor Arte of Warre Volume 2: The conduct of war in the reign of Elizabeth I, 1558–1603: Diplomacy, Strategy, Campaigns and Battles* Jonathan Davies

No 19 *The Kalmar War 1611–1613: Gustavus Adolphus's First War* Michael Fredholm von Essen

No 20 *Hojo: Samurai Warlords 1487–1590* Stephen Turnbull

No 21 *The Battle of Castillon 1453: The Death Knell for English France* Peter Hoskins

No 22 *The Tudor Arte of Warre Volume 3: The Conduct of War in the Reign of Elizabeth I 1558-1603: The Elizabethan Army* Jonathan Davies

No 23 *Sweden's War in Muscovy 1609-1617: The Relief of Moscow and Conquest of Novgorod* Michael Fredholm von Essen

No 24 *'Of Kerns and Gallowglasses': Irish Armies of the Sixteenth Century, 1487-1587* Robert Gresh

No 25 *'The Italian Wars Volume 5: The Franco-Spanish War in Southern Italy 1502-1504* Massimo Predonzani

No 26 *The Sieges of Rhodes 1480 and 1522* Jonathan Davies

No 27 *The Swabian War of 1499: The first confrontation between Landsknechts and the Swiss* Albert Winkler